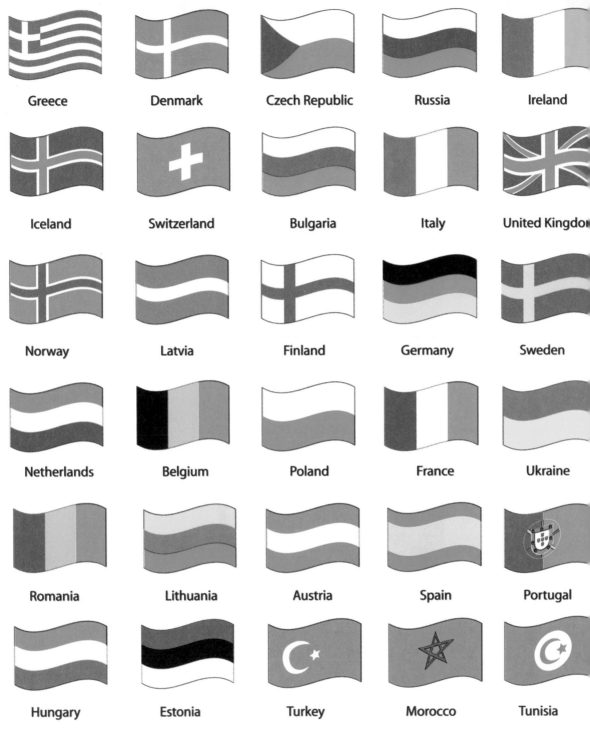

Greece	Denmark	Czech Republic	Russia	Ireland
Iceland	Switzerland	Bulgaria	Italy	United Kingdom
Norway	Latvia	Finland	Germany	Sweden
Netherlands	Belgium	Poland	France	Ukraine
Romania	Lithuania	Austria	Spain	Portugal
Hungary	Estonia	Turkey	Morocco	Tunisia

Megatrends Europe

Adjiedj Bakas

with Laura Schweig

Copyright © 2006 Dexter Communicatie BV

First published in 2006 by:

Marshall Cavendish Business
An imprint of Marshall Cavendish International (Asia) Private Limited
A member of Times Publishing Limited
Times Centre, 1 New Industrial Road
Singapore 536196
T: +65 6213 9300
F: +65 6285 4871
E: te@sg.marshallcavendish.com
Online bookstore: www.marshallcavendish.com/genref

and

Cyan Communications Limited
119 Wardour Street
London W1F 0UW
United Kingdom
T: +44 (0)20 7565 6120
E: sales@cyanbooks.com
www.cyanbooks.com

A CIP record for this book is available from the British Library

ISBN-13 978 981 261 834 4 (Asia & ANZ)
ISBN-10 981 261 834 1 (Asia & ANZ)
ISBN 1-904879-75-6 (Rest of world)

Printed and bound in Singapore

Contents

Guest columns

Every exit is an entry somewhere else.
Tom Stoppard

For Willem de Vries (1923–2005), my wise and humorous friend
and coach, who taught me that change is the main rule of life.

Foreword

Writing a book about European megatrends seems an almost impossible assignment. European countries differ from each other, and the differences between East and West are still large. There is a prosperity chasm between the two Europes that will not be bridged by the coming generations. Nevertheless, the mentality in East Europe is more positive than in the West: the previously sombre East Europeans have become undisputed progressive thinkers. An interesting detail here is that they do not take their European neighbours as their example; instead they look to the far-off United States which, in their eyes, gives better shape to the future. In Eastern Europe there is considerable enthusiasm for a capitalist future, instead of the feigned solidarity that is still common in Western Europe. It is exactly the opposite from Western Europe, where a certain amount of conceit is proving a major obstacle.

Despite the limitations, the reader has here a book that gives a sharp vision of Europe and its future. It is sometimes assured and accurate, sometimes more reticent, since certain trends do not allow themselves to be extrapolated to 2020 or further. *Megatrends Europe* contains an inspiring, fresh and sometimes humorous look at the Europe of today and tomorrow: a Europe that can never become "one" or a "federation of nation states", but a Europe that has enough social and cultural similarities to allow it to become a "community". Here the various cultures will remain, as long as they are clearly profiled. Exactly how this "many-nation-union" will develop is something only the future will tell.

This does not mean that we should allow the future to ambush us. Futurology, in the widest sense of the word, remains important, in both politics and business. Those who do not think about what they wish to achieve tomorrow will not be able to make any decision today. Trend-watching, a discipline fathered by futurology, is a useful aid in this, because the opposite is also true: who knows what they should do tomorrow if they are unaware of what is happening today?

Books such as Bakas' *Megatrends Nederland, Megatrends Europe*, and their predecessors *Megatrends Osteuropa* by Erich Obersteiner and Paul Putz, and *Megatrends Asia* by John Naisbitt, are thus important. They act as eye-openers. They show that we must look further than the end of our nose. They let us see things that we may have known but had not fully realized. They are books that instruct but also entertain. I hope this book will allow a combination of the education of Western Europe and the entertainment of Eastern Europe. Then things will turn out well.

Frits Bolkestein

Preface

"The present is big with the future," wrote Rudyard Kipling. And that is true. The future is already with us. We already see the first contours of the majority of the most important trends that will radically change Europe in the coming decades, although it is not fully obvious in every situation which of the possible future scenarios will become reality. We are actually living in a period of transition. There are already prototypes of several major technological developments that will come onto the market in the coming decades. In most cases, it is not commercially viable to put them into production. But they are near at hand.

For Europe, this will definitely be a century of transition. The old continent, which has long played a leading role on the world stage, will, in this century, have to accept the pre-eminence of India and China – known collectively as Chindia. At the beginning of 2005, China and India signed a "partnership of peace and prosperity". For many years, the countries were rivals rather than partners. They battled each other with words and weapons, and their border conflicts, which had previously caused the rattle of sabres, still continue. The Dalai Lama, for example, who fled from Tibet after China took over rule of that country, lives in exile in India, something that does not make China particularly happy. There is still a long way to go before both countries will become true partners, but this does little to detract from the importance of the agreement. If the leaders of a third of the world's population make agreements about cooperation, this has implications beyond Beijing and Delhi. In Europe, too, we shall have to realize that the self-awareness of these great Asian nations is growing and that the bundling of their economic strength and political know-how will have consequences for the world at large.

The economies of China and India are already partly responsible for trade and industry in the "old" continents of Europe and America. In the field of IT, the input of these countries is important for an increasing number of European companies, from the German Siemens to the Dutch Philips. And the Indian steel company Mittal is the largest company in its field in the world after its acquisition of the American International Steel Group. Mittal decides from India the welfare of steel factories and their workers in various continents. There are also plenty of examples for China. It is buying its way into various Western markets, such as IBM, and gives them a new meaning. China is responsible for the growth in transhipping in virtually every West European harbour, and Rotterdam in particular. And at the time of writing, Shanghai Automotive Industry Corporation, a China car manufacturer, has gained the keys to the survival of the British car factory MG Rover. More cars from Chinese and Indian manufacturers, such as the relatively unknown JMC brand, which offers a more favourable price–performance ratio than Western car brands, will appear on the market in the near future.

The tourist agreement between China and the European Union will see a growth in Chinese tourists in Europe. The same can be expected of India. Both countries will soon have a middle class twice as large as the whole European population. They will enjoy coming to Europe on holiday, and the streets will become increasingly Asian. The consequences of this flourishing relationship between China and India will be not only economic but also political. At the moment there are many obstacles that have to be overcome before they see any results of their exertions. The fact is that both countries are nuclear powers with increasingly modern armies. India has already suggested a permanent seat for itself on the Security Council of the United Nations. China can, if it chooses, be the logical advocate for this. A good working political axis formed by Beijing and Delhi would be a power bloc that cannot be ignored. It would be capable of changing the face of the world, and with it Europe. The European Union will have to set its sights increasingly on the East. Europe would do well to revive the slumbering European-Asian politics. A Chinese–Indian "partnership" is an extra reason to promote far greater cooperation with Europe. Integration of China and India into the world economy and the political structures connected with it is of strategic importance for Europe. Politics, economy and futurology form a cocktail that Europe in the 21st century cannot live without.

I am no futurologist. I make eager use of futurology and other disciplines, such as economy and philosophy. Trend watching and trend forecasting are both exceptionally interdisciplinary and multidisciplinary. You can only signal trends if you combine know-how from various disciplines and professions. As a trend watcher, I pay particular attention to how countries, organizations, people and the world change, and how resultant needs are thus changed, or how technological inventions change people's lives and lifestyles.

In this book, people have the central role. A book about the changes in the world and the new position of country, companies and people in it can perhaps be written in Europe. I have written various sections in various European countries. But it is my opinion that travelling not only expands one's own vision, it also makes a view of Europe more objective. That is why I chose to write a large part of this book abroad: a part in Montevideo, the capital of Uruguay, a part in the Argentinean capital Buenos Aires, and a part in the Asian cities of Shanghai, Hong Kong, Taipei and Delhi. In these last-mentioned cities, the rhythm of the new powerhouse Asia can clearly be felt. In the first two cities, there is a tangible feeling of reflection on a mighty past. Argentina and Uruguay belonged, 80 years ago, to the eight richest countries in the world; that is no longer the case.

This book describes, in an international framework, the seven megatrends that will radically change life in Europe in the coming decades. Being Dutch liberal, I describe these trends in a direct manner. Since the assassination of Pim Fortuyn and Theo van Gogh, in the Netherlands it's quite generally felt that everything one thinks can be said, even if it's just to keep the dialogue going. I wrote this book from this point of view. People might find it provocative and they might be offended. Of course that's not my intention. I just want to be an eye opener.

In my thinking about and forming of these trends, I have sought inspiration from various thinkers of a whole range of nationalities and their writings: John Naisbitt, Don Beck, Bernard Lewis, Karen Armstrong, Samuel Huntington, Francis Fukuyama, Gavin Menzies, Frits Bolkestein, Oriana Fallaci, Theo van Gogh and other important sources of inspiration. Various people have contributed to this book. They have helped sharpen my thinking. Eastern-European experts Ockje Tellegen, Caroline van Thessen, Karin Veldman and Tom Kuperus made important contributions to this book. In addition, Hans Ritman (Scriptum Publishers), Mirjam Sijmons, Liesbeth van Dijk, Frans van Rijn and Gerald Scharrer were of considerable value during its writing.

Critical readers were Vinco David, Peter Weijland, Minne Buwalda, Bert Knol and Wim de Ridder. They contributed valuable ideas and suggestions which were all to the good of the book. Laura Schweig was responsible for the editing of the Dutch edition. Former European Commissioner Frits Bolkestein wrote the introduction, and columnists from various countries made contributions to this book.

This book is based on various research programmes, books, lectures and other publications, many discussions with people from Europe and other continents, brainstorming sessions, personal observations and interpretations, and various projects and (field) studies that were undertaken in the past 16 years by our consultancy bureau Dexter.

Many thanks to everybody for their time, energy, knowledge, involvement and inspiration. Without them, this book would never have appeared.

Adjiedj Bakas
Amsterdam, January 2006

Dear readers, do you remember the year 2010, when China became an Empire again? And how delighted we were when the new Chinese Emperor married a European woman? Today she is back in Europe – Empress Cixi II of China is visiting Venice, where she will address European government leaders. Here are the speeches of the Empress and European President David Beckham.

President David Beckham, valued European commissioners and leaders of governments, we greet you with genuine joy. Unfortunately, the Emperor was unable to accompany me on this trip to Europe. The war in Iraq demands his presence in our capital Beijing.

We are pleased to be standing once more on European soil. We find it pleasing to be here with your courageous President who, since his entry into European politics at the time of my betrothal to the Emperor, has with persistent vision developed a liberal population policy. Europe is all the better for it. You have opened the continent to 4 million Chinese from the former Dutch colony of Indonesia, and thus you have afforded them new opportunities when they wished to flee the emerging Muslim fundamentalism in Indonesia. Similarly, the de-Saudi-ization of Scandinavia and Germany in recent years is cause for satisfaction, certainly after the emigration of European multiculturists to their new homeland, Saudi Arabia. President Beckham, with your Dutch European Commissioner Rita Verdonk and your Danish European Commissioner Anders Rasmussen, you have brought about a change in thinking, and you deserve our congratulations for that.

We are also delighted that European schoolchildren are now being taught the truth that in 1421, China discovered America, and that in 1492, Columbus used our maps of the world and knew exactly what he was going to "discover" in the West. We are also extremely happy that tomorrow we shall be opening the 1421 museum in Berlin, which will include a Chinese wreck among its

exhibits. Your highly capable experts recovered this wreck – one of the hundreds of ships that, under the command of eunuchs, made up the Imperial fleet of 1421 – from the Straits of Magellan in Argentina.

This week we shall be visiting a number of Chinese Europeans who now live in the Chinatowns of Cologne, Stockholm and Rome, and shall attend bicultural design shows during the Fashion Weeks in Milan, Paris, Amsterdam and Hamburg. In honour of Europe, where we were born and grew up, we are today wearing an imperial gown from Chanel, a fashion house that is much loved in Asia.

President Beckham, we are pleased today to offer Europe membership of CATO, the Chinese Atlantic Treaty Organization. We are also asking you to participate in the Chinese army in Iraq, which was sent there to quash the armed coup by Muslim fundamentalists, which the US army was unable to control. We also, naturally enough, have something to offer you. Parts of Europe are threatened by rising sea levels and the high levels of water in your rivers, such as the Rhine. New dykes are needed, but they will cost 300 billion. That is excessive for impoverished Europe. We are therefore offering development aid to finance the new dykes and dams. We also offer you assistance, in ways that can be decided later, in the matter of the threatened division of Europe into Eurabia and New Europe – something that could become imminent in the decade before us.

We are pleased to be able to officially open the new Chinese Embassy to the European Union in Brussels tomorrow. The old building had become too small to house our 3000 employees. We are also pleased, President Beckham, that in your second period in office, you are making use of a Chinese limousine.

We also praise the partner cities to Shanghai: Hamburg, Antwerp and Rotterdam, the most important habours in the European Union, and the main ports for the transport of Chinese products to the European Union. As you are aware, currently one in five of all industrial products worldwide is manufactured in China. We also invite you to share our joy in the fact that next week the first European will set foot on Mars, thanks to the Chinese spaceship *The Long March*.

We also offer our thanks to Europe for the entertainment it offers Chinese tourists. Europe is now one large open-air museum – a human zoo for our tourists – and we are delighted that the aesthetically disturbing concrete-block buildings are now being given a facelift with retro gables designed according to European traditions. Now, at least, our tourists will know that they are in Europe. We are also delighted with the fact that the Chinese-European film *Kung Fu 12* has become a hit in cinemas around the world.

We do have our concerns. The quality of Chinese language tuition in European schools is still lagging behind that of English. In the light of the economic power relationships, this is no longer acceptable. When I next visit here, I hope to be able to talk to many in Mandarin.

We wish you, in the spirit of Confucius, all the good that the Buddha teaches us, and place our trust in a continuation of our good relationships. Thank you very much.

Your majesty, our sincere thanks for your friendly words about Europe and myself. *Ni hao* – I bid thee welcome, I say to you now in Mandarin. Welcome to Europe, also on behalf of the royal families in those countries where the monarchy has been retained. Later in the week the monarchs of Spain, England, Sweden, Norway, Denmark, the Netherlands and Belgium look forward to welcoming you to a reception in Versailles. I also extend a welcome on behalf of the High Commissioner for Refugees, Gerhard Schröder. He is unfortunately unable to attend today, because of a refugee matter in the United States.

Your majesty, your mixed marriage is an example for many, including the many immigrants in Europe. Mixed marriage promotes integration under the motto "sleeping your way in". I hope that more Europeans will follow your example. That Europeans now live throughout the world, and many in China, is a positive development. Governing this diaspora is a core task of our European government and that of the regional governments of the EU countries. In this area, we have learnt a lot from China. We have given Europeans abroad voting rights in Europe, they can also enjoy our tax advantages, and we hope they will retain links with Europe and maintain their European feeling. China did this for decades before us. The Chinese diaspora was and is a network economy, which in 2005 already included 50 million people and was the third largest economy in the world

Your majesty, that you have come to visit us today, dressed in a European-designed gown is an enormous honour. I am pleased that you will be visiting various Fashion Weeks while you are in Europe. You underline the importance of creativity as a core value in Europe, as the Spanish politician, Roberto Navarro, stressed when he was European Commissioner in 2005.

I like the Chinese limousine a lot. I am also pleased that the Dutch European Commissioner Rita Verdonk and the Swedish European Commissioner Frida Lyngstadt (who became active in the European Elderly People's Party after her career as a member of Abba) are now also driven in Chinese limousines. The positive influence China has on our continent is enormous. As long ago as 2005, China financed the harbour expansions in Hamburg, Antwerp and Rotterdam, and thanks to the intensive sea traffic between these cities and Shanghai, there are many Chinese now living there.

I am extremely happy with the decision of the Chinese government to make gay marriage possible in China. You will be aware that European countries were the first in the world to do this.

I also understand that it was a pragmatic decision: Your one-child policy has resulted in an excess of men in China, and in those circumstances a gay marriage is quite practical. I am pleased that we have acted as a guiding continent. I am also pleased that your Yangtze river is once again navigable, thanks to the European dredging operations there. The marketing of Europe as a water-management continent has happily borne fruit. The first results can be seen here in Venice. The city used to be flooded regularly, but now thanks to an ingenious irrigation system, it always remains dry. We are also delighted that your government aircraft was built for you by the European Airbus Corporation.

I accept with humble thanks your development aid. You know that for Europeans there is nothing worse than wet feet. In the early years of this century, we noticed this when cities such as Prague and Dresden were flooded by the high waters in the Rhine. The new dykes in the sea and on the river banks will be constructed as quickly as possible. I also accept with thanks the membership of the CATO, the Chinese Atlantic Treaty Organization. A European fleet, under the command of the cruiser *HM Juan Carlos*, will sail tomorrow for Iraq to support the Chinese troops there.

Your majesty, I would like to propose a toast to you and all those present here today. To fruitful Chinese–European relationships, and to the future!

Introduction

It is the autumn of 2050. People in North-West Europe are sitting outside on a terrace. The temperature, thanks to climate change, has risen to such a degree that even in November it is quite pleasant to be outdoors. Nobody, however, is wearing summer clothes; that is no longer sensible. First, because the sun has become a much-feared enemy, and second, because the Islamic population – which, in the large cities, is now very much in the majority – does not approve of such things.

Many of the Europeans are 55 or older; young people have become an "endangered species". The seniors look very good indeed: botoxed, face-lifted, well dressed, immaculately groomed, and sporting trendy make-up. Brain-gymnastics and new medical research have eliminated memory loss and dementia; a chip implant in the brain prevents the decline that was so prevalent in the Europe of the past. These energetic seniors are really grown-up young people.

In the meantime, the clothing industry in Milan is struggling to supply the Chinese and Indian tourists and businesspeople with haute couture. They all come here in droves for a temporary stay, and are so prosperous and addicted to shopping that the designers and retailers have a hard job satisfying their needs. Italy earns quite a bit of pocket-money with it all. In Denmark, the fur industry – once large, now mega large – enjoys a growing demand from Asia.

Let's turn our attention to France or Poland. Imagine a primary school and listen to the chorus of voices. They no longer chant English verbs, but write Chinese characters and whisper to each other in Hindi. These are the traders of the future; they will service the trade relations with the Asian superpowers: bicultural, multilingual, cosmopolitan and metro-sexual.

Europe looks like one enormous Disneyworld for Asian tourists, a human zoo. The visitors gape at our typical architecture, some of it original, some not. The signs in the European tourist cities and the explanatory notes in museums are now also in Mandarin and Hindi, out of respect to the visitors.

The ever-expanding airport of Berlin – which was opened in 2015 to replace the city's various smaller airports – has become the hub for Chinese tourists. Chinese tour operators fly their passengers from all parts of China into Berlin, centrally positioned in Europe. From there, they swarm out by bus, airplane, and high-speed train to all corners of Europe. Scandinavia attracts many visitors, thanks to its natural beauty, fjords, mountains, characteristic architecture and modern design (glass, carpets, sculpture, furniture design). The huge hydro-generation plants have made the area one of the principal energy suppliers for Europe. If you listen carefully, you can hear the massive turbines growling on the sea-bed.

In the French and Italian countryside, which had become almost uninhabited at the start of the 21st century, there are now many houses used by European and Asian tourists in a broad variety of time-sharing schemes. Many Europeans now participate in "part-time living", and have houses both in the city and in the country. In this way, they live in two realities simultaneously. But the Asians, too, have rushed to sign up for a holiday home in Europe. The local shops now not only stock pasta and wine, but also curries and Peking Duck. In all European restaurants, you can eat with cutlery, chopsticks or – according to the ancient Indian tradition – with your hands. Dishes are available in different portion sizes, as seniors eat less than juniors.

England, Belgium and the Netherlands have adapted their entertainment industries to suit these new times. Architects have created spectacular modern buildings and also replicas of older buildings.

King Charles of England, who in the 20th century lambasted modern architecture, has been proved right. Many neighbourhoods dating from after 1945 – neighbourhoods characterized by dehumanizing, dull architecture – have been razed to the ground. This is also due to the drastic reduction in the population. In Germany, for example, there now live 10 million fewer people than in 2005.

Technology is everywhere, but has largely become invisible: cables and cable ducts have disappeared from houses, everything is cordless and connected to everything else by infrared. Similarly, television and sound equipment have disappeared. Televisions, computers and stereos are integrated into one unit, and music comes from virtually invisible speakers in the walls and ceiling. CDs no longer exist; everybody makes use of a digital library. There are no more window cleaners; windows no longer get dirty. They are covered in foil that contains enzymes that break down dirt. The paint used in houses also contains a dirt-destructive enzyme, and this makes cleaning and maintenance a lot simpler.

And then there's that strange border that runs through the former European Union. To the left of the border there is Eurabia; to the right, New Europe. To the left, the Muslims are essentially in control, even though they are in the minority. To the right live the original inhabitants of Eastern Europe, together with people from "old Europe" who do not wish to live under a Muslim government. Although they still regularly stay in their home countries, they live for the majority of the time in the Christian former Eastern Europe. Those people who insisted on staying in their home countries and have become citizens of Eurabia live in closely guarded Christian neighbourhoods. They cocoon a lot. At the weekend, they prefer to stay at home – either in the city or the country – and cook and chat with friends. There are many private security firms around that try to defuse the tension between the various groups. Apartheid has become the norm: in liberal enclaves, people of different convictions live together, but in other regions and city districts ghettoes have emerged. The tension between the non-Islamic groups and the Muslim rulers has increased to breaking point. The gap has never been greater. Terrorist activities organized by both sides are regular occurrences. Highly qualified liberal Muslims have left Eurabia and now live elsewhere in liberal enclaves such as Dubai, Oman and Malaysia.

Back to the present. Things all look very different from what we have just sketched, which implies that we have a few exciting decades ahead of us in which much will happen. Europe will get a new face. When the seven European megatrends that are dealt with in this book have taken place, Europe will have been totally transformed. But global trends will also be felt. Two international megatrends will play a role in the background: first, the emergence of a new economic world order, and second, the ongoing struggle between Islam and the West. These trends are discussed below. The seven European megatrends are handled in separate chapters.

International megatrend 1: new economic world order

The world economic, political and military power relationships were, for a long time, clear. After the end of the Second World War, two countries – the United States and the Soviet Union – were the only economic and military superpowers. The "cold war" raged between these two superpowers, and other countries chose one side or the other. After the Second World War, Japan developed into the second richest country in the world, but this was not translated into political, diplomatic or military power.

But the fall of the Berlin Wall and the disintegration of the Soviet Union radically changed this picture of the world. The United States became the only superpower. Japan remained the second richest country in the world, but it still did not have any military power. We now live in a unilateral world. The United States is dominant in the world in three areas.

The United States at the top

First, the United States is dominant in the economic field. It is the leading economy in the world. Its GDP is the highest in the world and the US economy has, for many decades, been the engine of the world economy. The lead is so large that it is expected to remain thus for the foreseeable future.

Second, it is dominant in the military field. The country must, whether it likes it or not, put out fires throughout the world.

The Americans have considerable difficulty in finding allies in their crusades against undesirable regimes such as that of the Taliban in Afghanistan and Saddam Hussein in Iraq. There was not too much difficulty with the first, since the attack on the World Trade Center on September 11, 2001 was seen as an attack on the whole Western world. In the second case, things were considerably more difficult; many countries did not recognize the necessity and this resulted in (to put it mildly) diplomatic unrest between the United States on the one hand, and Germany and France on the other. The United States generally takes the lead in such interventions, and this makes it the "world's policeman" and the greatest military superpower.

And finally, it is dominant in the cultural field. The American way of life is the lifestyle to which most people in the world aspire; it goes hand in hand with consumption. Hollywood is the most important exporter of American culture and its values and norms. Icons of culture such as Coca-Cola and McDonald's have a firm position throughout the world, often at the cost of local drinks and customs: in the majority of Asian cities, Coca-Cola has taken the place of tea. Just to be on the safe side, Coca-Cola has signed a contract with Nestea, so that they can now conquer the tea market.

The American ideal of beauty has become that of virtually the whole world. This ideal of the beautiful person is largely Caucasian-oriented: tall, lightly tanned (with or without the use of artificial tanning agents), slim (while in, for example, Negro and Asian cultures obesity is a sign of prosperity), with straight hair (whether artificial or natural), regular eyes (plastic surgery comes to the rescue here), sporty (while in some cultures, such as the Indian, sport does not play any role in daily life), wearing Western clothing (without any ethnic decoration) and relatively sober jewellery and watches. The related American behaviour means speaking English, moving quickly, walking and talking, speaking loudly (in contrast to the softer speech of, say, Northern Europe and South-East Asia), in your face, with the body language of a world ruler, emitting self-assurance, hedonistic–religious, self-aware and optimistic, lively. The body is seen as the temple for a progressively driven soul, and spirituality is used to define citizenship.

In the field of design, the American skyscrapers, mirror gables, light interiors, unfussy design, the use of concrete, steel, aluminium and glass as building materials, the way of infrastructural planning, and the vision of urban development lead the way. In virtually every city in the world, new office buildings erected in the last few decades are uniform and American-inspired. When you look around you at the new buildings in business centres, you are hardly aware of the city in which you find yourself.

The American film is the most important way of preaching American cultural values and beauty ideals to the world: Hollywood has thus become the cultural capital of the world. And the American ideal of beauty is adopted everywhere in the world: from Asia to Africa, skin-bleaching products are best sellers. In Asia, the operation to remove skin around the eyes so that they become more "Western" is extremely popular. Worldwide, tall people have better prospects of a good career than short people. A sporty lifestyle, fitness, jogging and maintaining a good physical condition (wellness) have become the worldwide norm, just as is a slim figure: slimming products and other methods of getting rid of excess fat are in great demand throughout the world, and the choice of Miss World and Miss Universe is annually made using the norms of American beauty. A century ago, Miss Ghana would have been a chubby little black woman; now she is a slim, light-skinned and straight-haired black woman. Miss India would previously have been a short woman of 1 metre 50, now she has to be at least 1 metre 70.

English is becoming the world language. If a French native and a Swede communicate, it is generally in English. Even when a Chinese and an Indian, a Brazilian and a Dutch native talk to each other, English is the language of choice. English words have been absorbed, adapted or not, into many languages. American pop music, which integrated many elements of black music such as blues, R&B and soul, has become popular throughout the world. At the start of the 21st century, Chinese pop music sounds American, and the same is true of modern Dutch, Indian and French music.

The United States on the decline

At the start of the 21st century, all this began to change. A world-wide discomfort with the way the United States fulfils its role as superpower is growing. Admittedly, it is impressive that in just two centuries, the most powerful country since the Roman Empire has grown out of nothing. Admiration and respect for this is certainly proper. But absolute supremacy without any real opposition leads to excesses and increased jealousy, something that automatically goes hand in hand with feelings of admiration.

At the start of the 21st century, America's image is no longer so good, a commission under the chairmanship of the former US minister for Foreign Affairs, Madeleine Albright, concluded. The war in Iraq has deeply divided America's allies. But while the attention of the world is directed at the war in Iraq, and to a much lesser degree Afghanistan, there is a revolution taking place internationally.

Do you remember the conflict between the United States and China that took place just prior to the memorable 9/11? The Chinese had brought down an American spy plane that had been flying over the Chinese coastline, and had dismantled it so that they could discover all its secrets. Instead of the world condemning China for bringing down the plane, people reacted indignantly to the American spy action. The Americans protested for weeks on end against the actions of the Chinese and refused to offer them their apologies. The Chinese, in turn, refused to budge an inch.

Ultimately the conflict was resolved, but the incident is symbolic of what is now taking place worldwide between the smokescreen of the wars in Iraq and Afghanistan, behind the conflict between Al Qaeda and the West. The United States still tops the league, but is seeing its power reduced on a variety of fronts. Other countries are growing stronger. Worldwide, a new economic order is emerging which will also overturn the current power balance. That is partly caused by the rekindling of Chinese ambition. China was a superpower earlier in its history (for example, during the Han, Tang and Ming dynasties), but time and again lost that position. In 1421, China discovered America and

Australia, as demonstrated by Gavin Menzies in his book *1421*. The Chinese carefully mapped out these continents – Columbus had those maps so he knew exactly what he would "discover" – but they never pushed ahead with the colonization of America and Australia. The world would now be a different place if they had. Napoleon once said, "China is a sleeping giant." That giant is now waking up.

Countries and (groups of) people in the world will, during the 21st century, regroup themselves as follows:

- superpowers
- tigers
- dormant countries
- raw material countries
- poor countries
- angry countries
- multinational organizations
- multinational tribes.

Superpowers

Superpowers are the most important economic and/or military players in the world, the countries which also supply the world with the

most distinguished scientists, inventors, technologists, artists and philosophers. In the 21st century, those countries will, according to the business bank Goldman Sachs, be the United States, (for the moment) Japan, and the so-called BRIC countries – Brazil, Russia, India and China. We shall thus have a world with six superpowers instead of one. Three of these six superpowers will be in Asia, which will mean that the 21st century will be characterized as the "Asian century".

Although the Russians are European, physically Russia is situated in both Europe and Asia. Culturally, it has, until now, generally associated itself with Europe. In the 21st century, that could quite likely change: Russia could turn towards the East, under the influence of economic relationships with Asia. Incidentally, Russia will be the smallest superpower, economically speaking. The Russian economy runs parallel to the price of oil, which makes the economy extremely one-sided; what's more, Russia is facing a serious decrease in its population. But the oil reserves in that country are so large that it will be able to earn a lot from them for some considerable time, not least thanks to the pipelines to China, Japan and India.

According to the same Goldman Sachs research, India will, by 2032, occupy third place on the list (it will by then have overtaken Japan), and China will gain the second place behind the United States by 2016. By 2041, China will have taken over the economic lead from the United States. It is now becoming increasingly possible that this will take place even sooner. The Goldman Sachs research dates from 2003; since then China has seen such enormous growth (a third of the world's production of steel is currently used by China) that 2041 now seems something on the late side.

In 2090, says *Jane's Defence Weekly*, China could also have surpassed the United States in the military field, were it not that China at the moment does not seem to have any military ambitions. The Chinese army is characterized by an entrepreneurial spirit: Chinese military are involved in business, own companies,

and already form China's largest multinational according to the American trendwatcher John Naisbitt. This is nothing new: it is simply the ancient Chinese clan system in a new guise.

Militarily speaking, things are rather different with India. For many decades, India has been at odds with its Islamic neighbour Pakistan. The two new nuclear powers have a stranglehold on each other, and India's position seems the weaker. Pakistan has acquired knowledge and technology for its own nuclear weapons from all corners of the world, including the Netherlands (via the nuclear spy Abdul Qadeer Khan and with Dutch help) and largely from Saudi Arabia and other oil rich countries. A remarkable fact is that China has made a considerable contribution. By helping Pakistan to develop nuclear weapons, China has manoeuvred itself into a stronger economic position than India. Because it does not need to involve itself in war, China can invest full-speed in its own economy. On the other hand, the conflict with Pakistan has made India's army the largest and most experienced in Asia at the start of the 21st century, and has made India the country best equipped to deal with terrorism. It has more than 50 years' experience with this. That experience could prove useful in the struggle for oil and raw materials. The (Islamic) countries near to China and India will most probably be the first to fall under the influence of one or other of these two superpowers, but in all those countries Muslim fundamentalism is an issue. India (with more than 150 million Muslims in a population of over 1 billion) has more experience and know-how in dealing with them than China, where there is but a small number of Muslim (Turkish-speaking) Uyghurs.

By the time that China rules the world we shall look back with nostalgia to our current anti-Americanism. The new superpower will (certainly in conflicts such as that in Iraq) act with a much firmer hand than today's United States. It is symptomatic that Mao Tse Tung is still respected in China, even though he put 50 million of his own people to the sword.

China: superpower in the 21st century or a repetition of the mistakes of 1421?

The 21st century will be the century of Asia. India and China will become new Asian superpowers; analysts are in complete agreement about this. But will China continue current trends? The Chinese economy has grown by approximately 10 per cent in recent years (by comparison, the Netherlands has grown by less than 1 per cent per year). According to various prognoses, by the middle of this century China will have overtaken the United States as the largest economic power in the world. China is currently the leader in a number of economic sectors. The country is already the largest producer of television sets. And it is not only in economic areas that the country is making an impression, but also in military and political areas. Large investments are being made in the army, and increasingly China is able to get its own way, whether it is about isolating Taiwan – China still considers that country a rebellious province – or agreements about the Spratly islands, which are claimed by a number of neighbouring countries in the South China Sea. China is a world power: several decades ago that was inconceivable, but now it is a real perspective. It is a perspective that is rooted in history. There were times when China was as rich and powerful as it would now like to become. The Chinese, inhabitants of the oldest existing kingdom in the world, have a long memory.

China as former superpower

The first era of China's world dominance lasted from approximately 200 BC to 200 AD, during the period of the Han emperors. China expanded and conquered parts of Korea and Vietnam, as well as areas along the Silk Route. This route was used for trade by other nations, including the Roman Empire. But it was not only silk that found its way to the West: other Chinese inventions such as paper and porcelain also found their way along the route.

In Europe we are taught about the might of the Roman Empire. Few of us learn much about China, which was just as powerful and prosperous in that period.

China flourished for a second time in a period lasting from the seventh to the ninth centuries, during the Tang dynasty. Europe had been thrown back into the dark ages, and China was superior in almost every field: economic, political, scientific and cultural. Printing – a Chinese invention – turned China into the first information society in the world. (There are still many in the West that believe that this honour fell, centuries later, to Gutenberg or Lourens Janszoon Coster.) Xian, the former capital of China, had around 2 million inhabitants and was thus by far the largest city in the world.

1421

At the start of the Ming dynasty, which lasted from the 14th to the 17th centuries, China attained a new level of power. All China's neighbours, from Japan to Siam (Thailand) paid tribute to the Chinese emperor. China was by the far the most powerful trading nation in the world. It had trading settlements along the Indian Ocean right into Africa. At the start of the 15th century, when the Europeans still believed that the world was flat, the Ming emperor Zhu Di had a mighty fleet of hundreds of sailing ships built in order to map the world. He wanted to trade not only in Asia and Eastern Africa, but also in countries that had not yet been discovered, so that they could be brought under his influence. In 1421 the fleet left China under the leadership of eunuchs (castrated men), the most faithful and loved allies of the emperor. The best cartographers, sailors and navigational instruments were on board. The fleet soon split up in order to discover and map various parts of the world. They reached the coasts of Australia, the South Pole, North and South America, and West Africa. They established settlements there and took away native plants and animals to offer as gifts to the emperor.

After two years of sailing and deprivation, the ships that had not been lost returned to China with a treasure of knowledge and maps of the whole world. But China had changed much in the meantime. The population was threatening to rebel against the astronomically high taxes needed to finance the fleet and the building of the new capital Beijing. To add insult to injury, a fire destroyed the imperial palace. Many believed that the gods were punishing the emperor for his arrogance in wanting to map the world and bring it under his power. In just a few years, China changed from an imperial superpower into an introverted giant which slowly fell asleep. World trade and distant expeditions became anathema. The maps and logs of the fleet were largely destroyed. Several maps reached the West by way of the Silk Route and were adapted there. They formed the basis for Columbus's "discovery" of America: thanks to the Chinese, he knew exactly what he was going to "discover". The knowledge that could have been used to secure world dominance was largely lost. Europe took over the baton, and European powers would rule the seas for centuries to come. European cultures would dominate the world until the start of the 21st century.

China in the 21st century

China is now on the return. The big question is how it will use its growing power in the 21st century. Will it this time be able to persist and become a superpower, or will it ultimately give up its imperialistic ambitions, as happened in the 15th century?

Brazil, in 2003 only the fifteenth economy in the world, follows a different strategy from China. Brazil is filthy rich with raw materials – raw materials that other countries are eager to have. The country has the largest concentration of Japanese outside Japan, and one of the largest groups of Germans outside Germany. These groups stimulate the economy, of which industry is an important pillar. Although Brazil, as eighth largest weapon exporter in the world, is involved in many of the world's problems, the country and its people are loved throughout the world. Brazilians are seen as harmless, happy party-goers, and they cherish this image. The expectation is that they will be able to retain this image, because they will make use of hydro power and obtain their oil from Venezuela. This allows them formally and politically to remain uninvolved in major conflicts. The conflict between Christianity and Islam is not relevant. Although there are many Muslims (mainly Lebanese) there, they are fully integrated and there is absolutely no inter-religion tension in the country. Brazil therefore has every chance of developing into a superpower. Whether this will actually happen is open to question: the economic recovery in the country has been predicted for some time, but has not yet happened.

Tigers

These are smaller countries with a strong economic foundation, characteristic talent management, ambitious, well governed, full of confidence, rich, but in size simply too small to play the role of superpower. The question is in which direction they will move. Tigers include Singapore, Chile, Vietnam, South Korea, Thailand, Turkey, South Africa, Poland and Canada.

Dormant countries

These are countries of varying size, with average prosperity. Some have reached considerable heights in the economic or cultural fields, but have now gone into decline. They are reasonably stable, with a population that is predominantly grey. They are not innovative, do not excel in any single area, perform averagely, live from investments made in better times, and are really nations that have gone into retirement. Their populations have few ambitions of making their country a world leader, and structures have rusted to a standstill. It is quite pleasant in them thanks to the peace and the stable political

climate. Examples of such countries are the Netherlands, Germany, Denmark, Uruguay, France, Sweden and Italy.

Raw material countries

The struggle for raw materials becomes, during the 21st century, the major struggle for everybody. Raw-material countries are countries that have deposits of one or more raw materials – mainly oil, iron ore (the basis for steel), coal and gas – and supply other countries, largely those from the categories already mentioned. These too are countries that excel in no single respect and simply live off the raw materials or process them. When raw materials play a key role, the governmental structure is largely feudal. Dynasties that long ago made themselves masters over these areas exploit them ruthlessly and do not stop at anything. Raw-material country Australia could be an exception to this because of its history. What's more, raw materials play a less dominant role in Australia than in, say, Kuwait and Ukraine. Other examples of raw material countries are Nigeria, Venezuela, Argentina and Libya.

Poor countries

These are countries that have little or nothing, where the largest part of the population live in poverty, afflicted by permanent lack of water, (civil) war, corrupt government, human rights contraventions and so on. These are countries such as Chad, Bangladesh, Myanmar (the former Burma), Congo, Somalia and Sudan. On the whole, they have few prospects.

Angry countries

These are countries that are permanently angry with themselves and the rest of the world. It is impossible to make them any less angry. They can be either rich (Iran, Saudi Arabia) or poor (North Korea), and what they nevertheless have in common is the injured mood in which they live. In fact, there is a mixture of perceived superiority and an inferiority complex. That these countries act as angry countries is sometimes supported by the population, sometimes not, and sometimes only partly. Since they are all dictatorships, it is difficult to estimate exactly how great the support is; objective sampling is never possible. Nationalistic arguments are often used to justify the anger.

Multinational organizations

Multinationals are now more powerful than many a country. These are companies that have their origins in one country (Philips in the Netherlands, Tata and Mittal in India, IBM and Microsoft in the United States, Siemens in Germany) or in several countries (Daimler-Chrysler in Germany and the United States, Shell in England and the Netherlands). A multinational is never nationalistic, and for the company national issues are less important than multinational issues. Multinationals have become superpowers which considerably influence decisions about life and work, economy and society in the countries in which they operate. The board of a multinational is often more powerful than a government. This is also true of other multinational organizations, such as the international accounts groups (KPMG, PriceWaterhouseCoopers, Deloitte and so on) and international environmental and non-governmental organizations (NGOs) such as Greenpeace and Amnesty International.

Multinational tribes

These are also not countries, but they certainly cannot be ignored. From time immemorial, people have belonged to "tribes", groups of people who share a language, culture and/or religion. These tribes have spread out over the whole world and have thus formed a diaspora. In most cases, a tribe settled on a particular piece of ground and formed a nation. Some countries were destroyed and the members of the tribe spread out to other regions. This was how the Jewish Diaspora came about after the decline of Israel in the first century of our calendar. In the same way, diasporas of Lebanese, Poles, Irish, Armenians and Kurds came into being. The Romanies also have a worldwide connection with each other. Some tribes never had a state, yet their commonality was sufficient, although spread over the world, to maintain an international connection with each other. Something such as this is true of the tribe of homosexuals (5 to 10 per cent of the world's population), even though the members do not share a language, culture or religion; they have settled in all countries of the world and maintain together a network economy. Tribe members of the homosexual tribe help each other worldwide in business.

The last few decades have seen a process of "new tribalization". A diaspora of 55 million Chinese has arisen throughout the world. Together, this group forms the third largest economy in the world: their collective GDP is 25 per cent higher than that of their 1.2 billion ex-fellow-compatriots in China. They rule the economies of Thailand, Indonesia, Myanmar, Singapore and Malaysia.

There is also a diaspora of expat Indians. They are called the NRI, the non-residential Indians, or PIOs, people of Indian origin. This tribe has a total of 20 million people with a combined wealth of US$340 billion. Annually, these 20 million people earn the same as the one billion people in India. The Indian government sees potential in this group and would love to bind these people to India, something that happens, for example, with fiscal benefits. The Indian government organizes annual diaspora conferences in Delhi, to which thousands of successful Indians living abroad are invited.

There are 7 million Americans living outside the United States, 1 million Bulgarians outside Bulgaria, an unknown but very large number of Germans or people of German origin living outside Germany (in countries such as Brazil, Argentina, East European countries and the Netherlands), 5 million Hungarians living outside Hungary, more Greeks living outside Greece than in Greece itself, and 3.5 million Turks in the European Union.

The most successful tribes are bicultural and multilingual. They are at home in several places at once and do not need a real homeland: they create in different places throughout the world a parallel society, cherish a virtual homeland, and live with parallel cultural structures. This is, incidentally, a new version of an old phenomenon: Coptic Christians have lived like this for centuries in the Islamic Egyptian society, and the same is true of the Jews in Islamic Morocco and Iran. People made use of informal communication infrastructures to maintain contact with the "homeland". In the middle ages, the hawala money transport system was created to send money to diasporas throughout the world.

Multinational tribes are a side-effect of globalization – tribe members spread out over the world – but at the same time create a new type of apartheid. In Churchtown swearing is prohibited; in

Little Arabia it is forbidden to sunbathe topless in your garden and a headscarf is obligatory for women; in Gaytown, open sexual behaviour is completely accepted and this in turn gives rise to excesses of hedonistic cultural life, including a rich artistic life and a red-light district; on the edge of the Goldcoast, you are frisked before you are allowed to enter.

During the coming decades, it will become clear how the relationships in the world will develop. Will the European Union become a third-world region? Will the United States become a dormant land? Will China and India take over world leadership, and what role will Brazil play? Will countries be disbanded or created to meet the needs of multinational tribes? The future will tell. In the meantime, another international megatrend will play a role, and the influence it has on the world will not pass unnoticed.

International megatrend 2: the struggle between the West and Islam

The 21st century will also play itself out in the light of the struggle between the Judaeo–Christian West and the Islamic world. The political commentator Benjamin Barber considers this a fight between unrestrained consumer capitalism on the one hand and religious and "tribal" fundamentalism on the other. It is a struggle between "logos" and "mythos", between mind and spirituality.

Spiral Dynamics consultant Peter Weijland sees the struggle as a conflict between feudalism and modernity. In his view, the conflicts of 9/11, 3/11 (the 11 March 2004 terrorist attack in Spain), 7/7 (the London bombings, 7 July 2005) and in the Middle East (Iraq, Israel) are not about the differences between Islam and Christianity or the consumer capitalism of Barber, but about a feudal (mainly Arabic) culture that is in the throes of transformation: the transition to modernity. In today's global world, Islam cannot remain as it is. It must renew and reposition itself.

The struggle, according to Weijland, is mainly taking place within Islam, although Osama bin Laden wants to place the blame on the external factors that have made transformation essential: the United States and the West. The dominant and arrogant attitude of the United States does not help create any milder image.

Weijland comments:

> You could say that power gods such as Arafat, Mubarak, Saddam Hussein, and the Assad dynasty in Syria, gain and use power in their own names while at the same time they undermine their own position with the ubiquitous opportunism, hedonism, and materialism of the West. This is exactly the conflict that Barber describes. In this conflict, it is not a question of whether Allah, Jehovah or God is the Almighty. Nor is it a choice between the Koran, the Torah or the Bible, although some people would like to push it in that direction. It is a crisis in the feudal world that is leading to enormous shifts in power.

It is, according to Weijland, all about power, not about truth. Others, such as the Mayor of London Ken Livingstone, place the blame on the West. The behaviour of the West in Islamic (oil) countries, such as supporting dictators, the wars in Iraq and Afghanistan, and the Israel–Palestine conflict, are supposedly the causes of the emergence of Muslim terrorism. The bad socioeconomic position of Muslims in Europe is also a bed for creating terrorism. That is nonsense. The socioeconomic position of Muslims in Europe is no better or worse than that of blacks, Latinos and other immigrant groups. The fact is that among large groups of European Muslims there has grown a culture of complaint. David Goodhart, editor-in-chief of *Prospect* magazine, has lambasted the culture of complaint (*The Guardian*, 15 July 2005):

> The overwhelming theme of public comment, even after the

recent bombings, is one of Muslim grievance. Britain's Muslims are among the richest and freest in the world and most of them are groping successfully towards a hybrid British Muslim identity, but when did you last hear a Muslim leader say so?

Goodhart concludes that the complaining persists, that an "explanation" is sought for what motivates the terrorists. An explanation is often found in "the war against Islam" that is being fought in Iraq by the United States and the United Kingdom. This is a stupid answer, says Goodhart. "How often do Muslim leaders point out that Tony Blair favoured ground-troop intervention on behalf of European Muslims in Bosnia and Kosovo?"

The British version of multiculturalism, which is also seen in Germany, Belgium, the Netherlands and other West European countries, is also severely criticized by Kenan Malik, a young British writer. He yearns for a recent past when immigrants from all corners of the world longed to feel British despite the discrimination that they felt. The multiculturalism that was preached by those in power put an end to that, he believes. The emphasis was placed on the minority as victims, particularly among Muslims. In *The Times* of 16 July 2005, Malik says:

> Muslims have certainly suffered from racism and discrimination. But many Muslim leaders have nurtured an exaggerated sense of victimhood for their own political purposes. The result has been to stoke up anger and resentment, creating a siege mentality that makes Muslim communities more inward-looking and more open to religious extremism – and that has helped to transform a small number of young men into savage terrorists.

British and other European Muslim leaders do not seem to understand what is expected of them, as shown by remarks made by Mohammed Naseem. He is the director of the largest mosque in Birmingham.

Naseem said, "Where is the evidence that four youths whose pictures were caught on CCTV cameras … were the perpetrators? How did we reject the possibility they were just innocent victims of this terrible happening? They had bought return train tickets." Feelings of victimhood in combination with leaders not interfering, can ultimately lead to terrorist acts. Of course, there are many kinds of Muslims, of which only a small part can be called radical or fundamentalist. In fact European Muslims can be divided into a number of categories:

- **MINOs:** Muslims in name only. They are formally Muslim, but in practice they have adopted universal humanist and liberal values and lifestyles.
- **Mainstreamers:** Average citizens with more or less the same values and norms as indigenous Europeans; they do not interpret Islam strictly and have little time for other Muslim variants.
- **Orthodox Muslims:** Strict in observance of the teaching, wearing headscarves, beards and turbans, but with more of folklore about it, they are satisfied with a status of apartheid in Europe. Often they are second or third-generation immigrants who, at a later age, have seen the light.
- **Complaining Muslims:** These lay the fault of anything that goes wrong in their lives on the fact that they are Muslim and "therefore" actively obstructed by non-Muslims.
- **Fundamentalists:** Either directly or indirectly under the influence of the Wahabi teaching, primarily expounded in Saudi Arabia and/or by Al Qaeda. Their aim is an Islamic colonization of Europe.
- **Converts:** These are indigenous Europeans, often from the lower classes, who have converted to Islam. These are, typically, the strictest followers of the religion.

It is expected that the fundamentalists will get a firmer grip on the other groups in the Europe of tomorrow. The French Muslim

expert Olivier Roy says that the strategy of the fundamentalists is clever and, what's more, funded by oil revenues. Their emergence in Europe cannot be stopped, with all the negative consequences this will have for Islam as a whole. For it's still a fact that the majority of Muslims don't want any conflict at all.

Andrew Wheatcroft, author of *Infidels*, which deals with the conflict between Christianity and Islam, says Muslim terrorism is propaganda for deeds rather than words. The Western wealth and lifestyle is attacked by this type of revolutionary violence. They wish to turn European society on its head. They are patient: religious enemies have all the time in the world. And, unlike our societies, long memories. The Muslim fundamentalism with which Europe is now struggling has its origins in a relatively new movement within Islam that is preached by people such as Said Qutb, the spiritual leader of the Muslim Brotherhood in Egypt, who was hanged in 1966. That movement reformed Islam. From today's perspective, the age-old conflict between Islam and Christianity has been in retrospect defined as a Holy War. Christianity and Islam fight for the same spiritual territory; they both assume that theirs is the real truth and that the other party is made up of unbelievers. They form each other's mirror image. If one had had its origins in Australia and the other in Iceland, it would never have come to a conflict. But now they confronted each other immediately after the emergence of Islam, first in the Middle East and then in Europe. History shows that living together is possible if both groups allow each other their faith. The problem is that many young European Muslims think it is not possible to live as a Muslim in a secular, multi-religious Europe. They believe that an Islamic life is only possible in an Islamic society.

Scenarios

It is important to ask how the new cold war, or rather hot peace, between the West and Islam will develop. The following scenarios are possible.

Scenario 1 *A century of power struggle*

The power struggle between these two blocs will continue throughout the 21st century. It will be fought with considerable violence, just as in the time of the Crusades, but now on a far larger scale. According to Barber, democracy will be the main loser at the end of this fight. This seems to me rather dubious: the new autonomy of European citizens and the independence of these citizens from institutes, states and authorities (partly thanks to the Internet) cannot, I believe, be negated. The struggle in the coming century can take four possible forms:

1   Islam wins and becomes the ruler of large parts of the world.
2   Christianity wins and prolongs its position of power.
3   Christianity and Islam unite and prepare for a fight against atheist China.
4   Christianity and China unite in the fight against Islam.

This last scenario seems the most probable: China and the Christian bloc have similar interests, including ensuring a free flow of oil from Muslim countries. Both blocs share progressive thinking and a preference for a liberal market economy, which is now manifesting itself in China. What's more, there are many similarities in the way China and the Christian bloc approach religion and spirituality. The Islamic Middle East is actually surrounded by China, India and Israel: three nuclear powers which share a common distaste of Muslim fundamentalism and will also (aggressively) combat it.

As long as the struggle continues, those places where Muslims and non-Muslims live together will be hotbeds of conflict. That is where the conflict is currently being waged: in Kashmir, Chechnya, Sudan, Israel/Palestine, Nigeria, Syria, Egypt, Indonesia, but also in EU countries, particularly those of Western Europe where large Islamic minorities live. This can in the long run lead to a new apartheid: because of the violence and mutual distrust, it will no longer be possible for Muslims and non-Muslims to live together, and governments will try to exchange their minorities. This was exactly how Turkey and Greece tried to reduce tension at the beginning of the 20th century. And it was also how Britain divided the Indian subcontinent into India (a country with a Hindu majority) and Pakistan (a country exclusively for Muslims). This form of "separated development" resulted in most cases in greater peace, stability and cooperation. In the recent European history, similar steps have been taken in the restless Balkan countries to separate the various groups living together and to cluster them in their own countries (Bosnia, Kosovo); such attempts have, until now, met with failure.

If there is an escalation in the conflict between Islam and Christianity, such repatriation initiatives can be expected. Where this does not happen, religious minorities will shut themselves off from the rest of society and withdraw into a parallel society. This will mean that many Muslims in Western Europe will withdraw into their own parallel society, liberal Muslims will leave Europe and settle in liberal Islamic areas, and Christians in Sudan will do the same. Contact will be maintained with like-minded people throughout the world using modern technology and new media (Internet, satellite television), and people will enjoy a virtual international community.

Scenario 2 *Defeating terrorism*

Experience shows that the life expectancy of most terrorist movements is between 12 and 15 years. That was true of the Red Brigades in Italy, the Baader-Meinhoff Group in Germany, the Enlightened Path in Peru and the Zapatistas in Mexico. Few terrorist organizations remain active for longer, with the exception of the IRA in Northern Ireland (which has now declared a cessation of all activities) and ETA in Spain. It is possible that Al Qaeda will be disbanded and that the conflict will quickly come to an end. In that case, we shall be able to breathe more easily. But that scenario is not probable. Al Qaeda is striving for an Islamic paradise on earth, based on the Sharia, the Islamic law. This is, according to the British historian and philosopher John Gray, a utopian view of the world that Al Qaeda leader Osama bin Laden hopes to achieve with terror. His Muslim fundamentalism and terrorism enjoys the support of about 1.5 billion Muslims around the world. The support for the Western terror organizations mentioned above was never this great. The international character of Al Qaeda makes the defeat of this organization in itself a utopian dream.

Exactly how great the support of European Muslims is for Al Qaeda cannot be calculated with any accuracy. Security services in all European countries where Muslims live have signalled a growth in Muslim fundamentalism, particularly among well-educated and apparently fully integrated Muslims. Liberal Muslims are being threatened by them, and keep quiet or leave Europe. There is a clear migration of well-educated liberal Turkish young people from Western Europe to the more liberal Istanbul.

There is also the suspicion that religion is not the main motive for many Muslim terrorists. On the contrary, the attraction is the financial rewards that are on offer. In the world of terrorism, a huge amount of money passes hands, and people want to take their share. As long as the money continues to flow, international Muslim terrorism will continue to flourish. It is simply too rewarding to be stopped.

Scenario 3
Turkey becomes the leader of the Islamic world

The next possibility is that Turkey will become the leader of the Islamic world. Serious thought is being given to this by the Turkish elite, and the idea is not as crazy as it may seem. Turkey has everything to become the leader of the Islamic world: an economy that is becoming ever stronger, a good and relatively democratic government, and a strong army. It has a long experience, stretching back over many centuries, in ruling a multicultural Islamic empire: the Ottoman Empire. And Turkey maintains close links with Turkish-speaking states that were previously part of the Soviet Union, such as Turkmenistan, and with the Turkish-speaking community in China, the Uyghurs. The country already forms a strong economic and cultural union with these countries and groups. Turkey therefore has experience in working together in a union, something that other Islamic countries do not have.

Certain conditions will have to be met: Turkey will have to reintroduce Arabic writing, and to bring back Arabic and Persian words that have been purged from the language. And the caliphate, the autocratic constitutional form that does not separate mosque and state but unites them, would have to be reintroduced. This would in principle make it impossible for Turkey to join the European Union (in all EU countries, church and state is separated), but there are voices of dissent: the Dutch historian Arend Jan Boekestijn maintains that the gradual erosion of the secular model can lead to restricting Muslim fundamentalism and therefore to a greater tolerance of minorities. That makes links with Europe much more natural. Boekestijn believes that fundamentalism is actually encouraged in a secular state because the state is constantly interfering with the religious convictions of its citizens. In an Islamic society, says Boekestijn, this is unnatural.

A partial "re-osmanization", the reintroduction of the system under the Sultans, is desirable for Turkey, since it will also give it a better position in the Islamic world. Reintroduction of the caliphate is part of this process, as we have already mentioned. Until the beginning of the 20th century the caliph, the spiritual and temporal leader of the Muslims, lived in Istanbul. Kemal Atutürk, the founder of modern Turkey, dispensed not only with Arabic writing but also with the caliphate. Their reintroduction is a thorny issue with the Turkish elite, who still cherish Atutürk.

If Turkey chooses to reinstate the caliphate and finds a way of immunizing itself against the rich fundamentalists of Saudi Arabia, it could become the political and spiritual leader of the Islamic countries. The Turkish elite are already discussing the Ottoman Union. Such a union would, of course, be given a different name; the associations with the old Ottoman Empire are too ostentatious. With the formation of such a union, Turkey would be able to crush Muslim fundamentalism and make sure that the area developed in a positive way. The various countries could remain independent, although that would not help the majority of them. Recolonization by Turkey or another country is essential to instil progressive thinking and development in a culture that has stood still for centuries. In the Middle East, a number of enlightened despots, such as Sultan Qaboosh of Oman and Sheikh Maktoum bin Rashid Al Maktoum of Dubai, have been able to show and realize such progressive thinking. Malaysia (under ex-Prime Minister Mahathir Mohamed) and Brunei are examples of well-governed Islam countries outside the Middle East. The majority of the remaining Islam countries fail in their government. In Turkey, however, the modernity of Atatürk has reigned for nearly a century.

A disadvantage is that Turkey does not have the enormous capital that the Muslim fundamentalists have at their disposal, capital that comes from the oil-rich Saudi Arabia, the source of Muslim terrorism. A second disadvantage is that Turkey, in contrast to the period of the Ottoman Empire, no longer has the three holy places of Islam (Jerusalem, Mecca and Medina) within its borders. When this was the case, it only strengthened the moral leadership of Turkey in the Islam world. Because of these two facts, it is unlikely that Turkey will be able to gain leadership over the Islamic world, which thus makes this scenario improbable.

In January 2005, the US National Intelligence Council, a think-tank of the CIA, published a report containing four scenarios for 2020, of which the most radical, and for me the most plausible, was one entitled "A new caliphate". The scenario is written in the form of a letter dated 3 June 2020 from Sa'id Muhammad, the fictitious grandson of Osama bin Laden, to his brother. In this letter, Sa'id Muhammad describes the situation in the world after the reinstatement of the caliphate. It is chaos. Parts of Russia, the Middle East and Africa have joined the caliphate. But in countries where globalization has made its mark, the Muslims are not so eager. The struggle between Shi'ites and Sunnis has become more virulent. Iraq, where a fragile peace reigns, has become a terrorist centre, the new Afghanistan. America is paying Russia to fight the Mujahideen. Despite the existence of the state of Palestine, things are still tense in Israel. But the grandson of the world's most wanted terrorist has hope. He considers the arrival of the caliph, the new successor to the Prophet Mohammed, as the salvation of Islam. With a caliph at their head, Muslim countries could blow up Western countries and bring the world under the will of Allah. And yet, in 2020, little of this has come about. "Grandfather would have felt enormously frustrated," sighs his grandson.

Scenario 4 *Eurabia and New Europe*

The fourth scenario is, along with the first, the most probable. Western Europe merges with the Maghreb to create Eurabia, and the former Eastern Europe emerges as the non-Islamic New Europe.

Western Europe is forced to give up its struggle against Islam and during the 21st century converts to Islam, something that has been predicted by the American Islam expert Bernard Lewis, the murdered Dutch filmmaker Theo van Gogh, and the Italian writer Oriana Fallaci. The conversion of Western Europe to Islam has a number of reasons.

Christians in the Western European countries are growing old. The youth is predominantly Muslim, particularly in the larger cities. Traditionally, the cities are the economic and cultural engines of the country. Once the cities fall into Islamic hands, then people have de facto power in their hands over the whole country, even if they are demographically still in a minority. This happened, for example, in India, where Muslims ruled for centuries, even though they only made up 10 per cent of the population.

A compounding factor is that the children and grandchildren of Islamic immigrants have a high level of aspiration: they are generally hard workers, assiduous students, ascetic, with a large degree of self-discipline and a readiness to sacrifice themselves. They frequently come from a deprived background, from a rough and tough capitalist culture, are used to using their elbows, and are far from soft (in contrast to indigenous children). While indigenous children fill their spare time with their Playstations and watching television, Islamic children have to play interpreter for their often illiterate parents, do extra school work, and learn things that indigenous children consider normal (local customs, culture, codes of behaviour). They have to find their own way in the religious and cultural maze they have landed in. In many areas they have to become self-sufficient, full of initiative and assertive. This makes them more streetwise than indigenous children, and they have more capacities for taking over business, politics and other areas from those just about to retire than indigenous children.

Another thing is religion. Muslims are strong believers, Westerners are generally not. One cannot fight fundamentalism with atheism. However, Europeans are experiencing a religious revival, although it is clearly separate from traditional churches and denominations (see Megatrend 3). The number of agnostics and atheists is decreasing just as is their influence, and (partly to set themselves off against the rising Islamic influences) more people are believing in "something" between heaven and earth. But this again is too weak and too vague to offer resistance. The "away with us" mentality now reigns in many European countries, together with an exaggerated fear of being thought racist or discriminatory. In addition, most forms of nationalism that exist in Europe are considerably weaker than Islamic solidarity. Admittedly, French nationalism is of all those in Europe the most intense. No wonder then that it was here that the anti-headscarf law was adopted, which forbade the wearing of headscarves in schools. This law was echoed in several German states, but in most other European countries it is not under discussion.

There is an increasing degree of Islamization on the streets. In various areas of Amsterdam, Antwerp, London and Paris it is almost impossible for a woman to walk along a street in a summer dress that exposes her shoulders without being called a whore, or without being aggressively hustled by Islamic men and women. The liberal Islamic French Iranian Chadortt Djavann wrote about this in a revealing way in her book *Take off the Veil*. Liberal Muslims in Western countries who want to integrate Islam are faced with threats from fundamentalist groups, and receive surprisingly little support from the indigenous population: Ayaan Hirsi Ali in Holland, Asra Nomani in the United States, Irshad Manji in Canada, Samira Bellil (d. 2004) in France, and the Turkish Necla Kelek in Germany.

Imams and other Islamic leaders who preach hate, anti-Semitism and contempt for European indigenous people are left alone under the guise of "freedom of speech". An example of this is the tour in London in August 2004 of the Egyptian fundamentalist Sheikh Yussuf al-Qaradawi, who in the name of multiculturalism was feted extensively by Mayor Ken Livingstone. Fundamentalists are not punished, or punished only lightly, because European legal systems are not equipped to deal with terrorism. Websites and television stations that preach hate – often based outside Europe – are accessible under the guise of "freedom of speech". France is one of the few countries that has taken Hezbollah television – a station that sows hatred – off the air.

The Islamic takeover of Europe has already started and seems extremely probable. The expectation is that most indigenous Western Europeans who still live here when it happens will simply accept it without protest, with the possible exception of the French. The Western European countries that fall under the rule of Islam will, to all intents and purpose, be annexed by the North African countries, and the actual union of Eurabia will be a fact.

In Middle and Eastern Europe, we shall see at the same time the emergence of New Europe. The US Secretary of Defense, Donald Rumsfeld, made a distinction in a speech he gave not so long ago between the old and the new Europe. He considered the traditional Western European countries to be part of old Europe. He reckoned the Eastern European countries (some of which are already members of the European Union) to be the new Europe. Germany, thanks to the reunification of East and West Germany in 1990, has a foot in both Europes.

In a lecture he gave to the Humboldt University in Berlin, Dutch thinker Frits Bolkestein urged a re-evaluation of the old Danube monarchy, the double monarchy of Austria and Hungary which existed between 1867 and 1918. In an impressive way, a multicultural Christian kingdom was held together, governed, and brought to great heights. The success factors for this double monarchy have, according to Bolkestein, even greater relevance today than they did then, and according to him we would benefit from implementing them in the 21st century.

We could combine the ideas of Rumsfeld and Bolkestein. The new Europe (Christian) would have to be founded on the constitution and geographical area of the old double monarchy, and Germany would have to become part of it.

That is an interesting idea. Eastern Europe is becoming greyer even faster than Western Europe, and Germany too is becoming greyer faster than other countries. How can this part of Europe, which is so predominantly grey, be revitalized? If that doesn't happen, then the area (whether or not united) will become a collection of dormant nations and will see a rapid decline in both economic and political influence.

Emigration by young and older Christians (including humanists, atheists, agnostics and others) from the countries in Western Europe that are becoming increasingly Islamic to Germany and East Europe would be able to provide a powerful stimulus for this area.

In addition, Germany, Poland and other Eastern European countries will have to invest in diaspora management. There are many people of German origin who live outside Germany (for example, in the future superpower of Brazil) and the Polish diaspora is also extremely large (people of Polish origin live in the United States, Australia and many European countries). Using these diasporas and investing in their virtual homeland feeling will prove beneficial, as the experiences of China and India with diaspora management have clearly shown.

In this scenario, the present European Union will be dismantled. Western Europe will become Islamic and will unite itself economically, politically and culturally (although not necessarily governmentally) with North Africa and Turkey, so they will together become Eurabia. In Middle and Eastern

Europe, there will arise a New Europe, where non-Islamic migrants from Western Europe will find their salvation. With Berlin/Vienna as its capital, it will be a religious, political, cultural and economic union, perhaps but not necessarily united under one government. This New Europe can make links with the raw-material nation Ukraine and future superpower Russia in ways that can be filled in later.

Which of these options will turn into reality is difficult to predict with any certainty. Taking into consideration all the possibilities and weighing up the pros and cons, it seems most likely that Western Europe will be turned into Eurabia and that a New Europe will arise on the geographical area of the Danube monarchy (scenario 4). In the meantime, the struggle between the West and the world of Islam will continue (scenario 1) and will take the form of a struggle between Christianity and China on the one side, and Islam on the other.

Nostradamus had a prediction for us in this area. According to him, around this time we will see arrival of the third Antichrist – the first two were Napoleon Bonaparte and Hitler – and this one will probably come from the Middle East. The result will be a bloody war that will cost the lives of two-thirds of all Europeans and three-quarters of all Muslims. Who this "Mabus" (as Nostradamus called him) will be is something we do not yet know; it could, of course, be Osama bin Laden. However Nostradamus warned that his future visions were not supposed to be taken too seriously. Human beings can always change the ways of history and learn from the past. I myself don't believe there will be a big war for the next fifty years. We will experience tensions, terrorist attacks and guerillas, but war? I don't think so. The fact does remain, though: we have some tense times ahead.

The European population shrinks and takes on new colours

Introduction

Despite the various signals given off by various European countries that Europe is "full", the opposite is in fact true. Europe is not full; the population may continue to grow for two decades, but after that it will decline. Eurostat, the office of statistics for the European Union, has outlined three scenarios for the future of Europe. In the first scenario, the population undergoes a rapid growth, largely due to mass immigration. This, however, is highly unlikely since there is little acceptance within Europe for further immigration from countries outside Europe.

In the second scenario, the population in Europe remains relatively stable. That is, of course, if European women put an end to their "birth strike" and go back to producing as many children as, for example, their American counterparts. In the third, and most plausible, scenario of Eurostat, the European population shrinks by between 23 and 40 per cent. This will be true if fewer children are born than the 2.1 that are needed as replacements. And this is currently the case.

The third scenario, a shrinking of the population, will most probably come about, and that is not a bad thing. We have, after all, experienced it before in Europe. Two thousand years ago, the city of Rome had more than 2 million inhabitants, but in the Middle Ages, there was a period when only about 200 (!) people lived there; now it is back to 2 million. After the First World War (1914–18), so many young French men had lost their lives that the population growth in France was seriously affected. And yet France become a powerful country in the 20th century and led the way in Europe (despite the recent "non" to the EU constitution).

As the European population shrinks, it will also take on new colours. We see more ethnic-minority tourists, which gives a more multi cultural street picture, and the immigration policy of the last decades has changed much in compilation of the European population. And although the immigration policy of "Fort Europe" is changing, with Denmark and the Netherlands leading the way, the tide cannot be turned. Europe is getting greyer, with fewer younger people, and at the same time more colourful. Have you ever driven on a motorway behind an 80-year-old grandmother? Get used to it – that is Europe's future.

Fewer and different people in Europe

Population growth and also population shrinkage are caused by three factors: birth rate, death rate and migration. The first two factors are such that Europe is shrinking. With just 1.37 children, the European woman has the lowest fertility figures in the world.

Women want pleasure and a career, and children just do not fit in with this. Because more and more women enjoy higher education, the expectation is that the birth rate will not increase; it is more likely to drop further.

Birth rate

If we look at the birth rate in Europe, we see considerable variation. In the Netherlands and France the figure is still relatively high: there, 1.7 and 1.9 children respectively are born to each woman. But other countries show an extremely low fertility rate: it is 1.26 in Poland, 1.15 in Spain, 1.23 in Italy, and 1.37 in Germany, which, at the same time, is also the average for the whole of Europe. For comparison, Africa has a fertility rate of 4.6. Because there is such growth in developing countries, Europe's percentage of the world population is falling. In 1900, a quarter of the world's population lived in Europe. In 1950 Europe, with 547 million people, accounted for more than 20 per cent of the world's population. In 2000 this had dropped to just 11 per cent, with 728 million inhabitants. If this trend continues, by

2050 the European population will be 632 million – just 7 per cent of the world population.

The decline in the European population has already started. In some countries it is yet to happen, in others it has been taking place for some time. The Netherlands, for example, has a relatively high birth rate and a young population, so the decline is not expected to start until 2035. Germany is currently relatively stable, and the real decline is expected to begin between 2010 and 2015. In Italy, the population is already shrinking, and this is also true of Poland.

Prognosis for the European population until 2050 (in million citizens)

Year	Population
2005	725
2010	720
2015	713
2020	705
2025	696
2030	685
2035	674
2040	661
2045	647
2050	632

Source: http://esa.un.org/unpp

Death

If the average age at which we die increases, thanks to medical treatment, the population will decline at a slower rate. But if elderly people die earlier (perhaps because of a flu epidemic) the decline will be faster. Probably we will be confronted in the future with new diseases, such as SARS and AIDS in the past. But let us be honest, a mass death of the elderly is not something that is very likely.

Because we are all living longer, Europe is the "greyest" area in the world. The average age of Europeans has risen from 29.2 years in 1950 to 37.7 years in 2003. According to a prognosis by the United Nations in 2003, this will rise to 47.7 years. The regional differences are large. In Northern and Western Europe the average age in 1950 was 34 years, while in Eastern and Southern Europe it was 30 years. In 2003, these figures were respectively 38 and 37 years; in 50 years, Eastern and Southern Europe will be so "grey" that the average age will be 50 years compared with 45 years in Northern and Western Europe.

Migration

Ethnicity is by far the most important theme in 21st century Europe, even if many politically correct types do not wish to know this. In Denmark, prime minister Anders Fogh Rasmussen won two successive general elections thanks to his strict immigration policy. In the UK migration was the most important theme in the 2005 election campaign, but this was also true of the French presidential elections in 2002, and in the Netherlands it has been the major issue in two consecutive elections.

In certain parts of London, whites are in the minority. This is the result of both non-white immigration and "white flight", a survey for the *Guardian* concluded. The British organization Migrationwatch reported that in Britain the white and ethnic communities were growing ever farther apart. "Segregation is a growing reality in British cities," wrote the *Sunday Times*. Migrationwatch claimed that, in the past few years, several hundred thousand whites have left the cities of Birmingham, Manchester and Bradford. They have been replaced by immigrants from Asia; in the last ten years, their number has doubled in the cities mentioned. The figures for London are even more remarkable. In the past few years around 606,000 people, mainly white, left the city, and 726,000, mostly immigrants, took their place.

What is taking place in the UK is being repeated in other countries. The level of immigration will continue, because immigrants are attracted to cities, while whites move to the countryside, and the elderly move abroad.

The decline in the population and the levels of immigration in Europe will radically change the continent. The consequences are considerable in a wide range of areas. We will deal with the consequences of decline here; the consequences of multi-ethnic immigration will be handled in Megatrend 7.

Consequences of the population decline

Housing

The emptying of regions is no new phenomenon. Europe has known many such periods of decline in the past: the countryside in France, Spain and Ireland emptied in the 19th century, for example. Geographical shifts of important trade routes also resulted in the past in a decline in certain areas, for example the old Punta Arena on the Straits of Magellan, Chile, which lost its role with the construction of the Panama Canal, and Kutná Hora in the silver mining region of the Czech Republic, which was at one time the second city in the Bohemian Empire.

A decline in the population has a number of advantages. Fewer people means less strain on the environment and lower energy and water use. There is more space per head of population, and that is a blessing. But there are also negative aspects to population decline. European countries focus on the growth function in such a way that long-term investments come under threat when the social costs for them have to be borne by fewer people. The advantages of economy of scale decrease, which means that the bills governments run up for municipal projects have to be footed by fewer people. Rents and the cost of energy and water are then increased. Tax income decreases and there is not enough money for new developments. This is at the expense of those people that remain. They are the main victims of the decline process.

East Germany has a special history, and it is therefore difficult to compare it with other declining regions in Europe. Here, it is not only the rural areas that are emptying, but also the cities. The speed with which this is taking place is remarkable. For example, in the new city (in German, Neustadt) of Guben-Spruke, on the outskirts of an old industrial city in the Lausitz, a traditionally agrarian region in South Brandenburg, 80 workers leave every month. Because of this, the population has halved in the last 50 years. The Lausitz became an industrial region following political pressure in the German Democratic Republic (GDR), and grew to be a supra-regional energy centre for the GDR. Because of the enormous growth in the area, the use of industrial building processes became essential. The result was *Plattenbausedlungen* (prefabricated panel building): independent living complexes with a modern level of appliances, certainly by the standards of the time. They had hot water and central heating: things that were not available in the old cities. Thanks to this, the new housing was in great demand. The advantages of these new cities were clear to both urban planners and architects. Thanks to a combination of a

high building density and an efficient infra-structure, the actual area on which the buildings were constructed was kept to a minimum, and there was a lot of green space left. The intended facilities, however, were frequently insufficient, or left out because of cost considerations, and the outside areas (and the planting) were seldom completed. After the fall of the Berlin Wall in 1989, the economy in the region collapsed and many people left to move to the west of the country. Because of this, Lausitz is one of the most rapidly shrinking areas in Europe. In 2001, 12.5 per cent of all housing in Brandenburg was empty.

The population shrinkage will not only take place in Germany. French and Italian rural areas are depopulating at a fast pace. In Italy, I have seen villages that used to boast 1000 inhabitants and now have just 20. The rest of the houses are boarded up. Because so few people live there, there are ever fewer shops: fewer bakers, grocers, super-markets, petrol stations, and also fewer schools and nurseries. Of course the Italian countryside has the advantage of breathtaking beauty. The joyless new cities of East Germany beg to be demol-ished. These picturesque little Italian villages demand new types of living concepts. They might offer part-time living, as a country retreat for city-dwellers from all parts of Europe, or provide country residences for Chinese, Indians, or people from other strong economies. The village of La Palombara in Italy was deserted by all its inhabitants in the 1970s. Now city people have moved in, eager to escape the incessant noise of traffic occasionally. They are called bio-regionalists. They do not stay for great lengths of time, because the sound of the wind becomes irritating. There will be more about part-time living in the future in the following chapters.

So far various governments have provided subsidies to alleviate the worst problems caused by this depopulation of rural areas (and East German cities), but that will eventually stop. You can only spend a euro once. What's more, all these subsidies do not lead to a structural, visionary solution. The expectation is that in Europe, now that the shrinkage in the population is so drastic, within the foreseeable future uniform, decisive measures will be taken. Then it will no longer be enough to demolish unattractive flats of Stalinist design and replace them with municipal parks. Then semi-abandoned cities will no longer become a Gruyère cheese, with flats and holes where flats used to stand. Then whole cities will be razed to the ground and be replaced with areas dedicated to nature. Or they will have an "entertainment" function for European tourists or for those from other countries, for example from countries in Asia. Then, of course, local inhabitants will have to become more positive and less xenophobic towards foreign visitors, but there is much to be gained by that: it is, after all, about trade and employment, and for that people are generally prepared to reach some compromise. The buildings that replace those in the east of Germany must be German in origin: replicas of former German architecture, or retro-building. That is timeless, and non-European tourists will know that they are in Germany. In France and Italy, the countryside has retained its authentic character to a much greater degree than in East Germany, and people find it charming. Renovation and a good brush-up will be sufficient.

Infrastructure

A good infrastructure is still necessary, but it will be used less intensively, which means that the costs per capita will rise. The same is true of electricity and drainage. Laying and maintaining roads will cost the same as before, but these costs will be carried by fewer people. It is essential that these people earn more in order to be able to pay for it all. The paradox is that in this century, Europeans will work less. A smaller group of people will earn more money for shorter working hours in order to foot the bill for the infrastructure in rural areas. How we shall do that, or rather how we should do that, will be discussed in Megatrend 6.

Parking will become an even more important issue than it already is in municipal planning in the modern Europe. The "rush-hour family" will become the cornerstone of society. The family will take care of partner(s), friends, extended family, children and elderly parents. Combining all this will demand mobility. Most European cities adopt a car-discouragement policy, however, and that is understandable. But how is, say, a working mother of 40 supposed to get around with her kids, their toys, her shopping, and her elderly parents without a car? Policies to discourage or prevent car usage will have to become more nuanced in the future as demographics and lifestyles change. Otherwise an increasing number of middle-class people who belong to the group of rush-hour families will leave the city and move to the countryside. They will then take urban cultural habits with them, so that the rural districts will also become more urbanized. There will be a growing market in Europe for cheap cars, most of which will be imported from China and India, all aimed at greater mobility for the rush-hour family.

Employment

The grey pressure is increasing: fewer young people must care for a growing number of elderly. There will be more than enough work in the future. Young people do not have to worry about mass unemployment. The whole entertainment and care industry for the elderly and for tourism will offer more than enough work. For a continent that will be made up partly of retirement countries (Western Europe) and partly of production nations (Eastern Europe: manufacture and services) and which will have fewer young people, this is a challenge.

In order to ensure that all this work is done, a part will be taken over by computers and robots. We shall shortly have computers that are ten times as intelligent as people, and these will be able to take over the work done by people retiring, so that the scarce group of young people will not have to work excessively hard. And we shall also, of course, see more robots like those that, in recent years, have taken on a lot of factory work (and don't complain about hours or pay, and never call in sick).

We shall also see the return of working animals. Recently, a television programme showed how a trained Alsatian virtually took complete care of a handicapped woman. The animal collected her newspaper and shopping, helped her shower and dress, and was also a caring companion – but with more hair than the companion ladies of the past. A dog like this can last for 14 years without any wage increase and is virtually never ill. In other words, it is a blessing for a person needing care.

The working population will thus be made up of young people, computers, trained animals and, of course, robots. In this way it is possible for a limited number of people to achieve a high level of productivity. This will be despite the greying, the decreasing number of young people, and the shrinkage in the population as a whole.

Care tourism

The care industry will profit from the growing number of elderly. People cost much more in the last ten years of their lives than in their preceding 60–70 years. These costs will drop, by the way. Medical technology is improving, and the elderly are more frequently adopting a healthy lifestyle. What's more, an increasing number of the elderly no longer accept ailing all the time: no lengthy deterioration and illnesses, dementia, and other health problems which not only decrease the quality of life, but also form a burden for those around them. Who really wants their nearest and dearest to remember a demented, incontinent, incoherently babbling man or woman?

More and more seniors will choose to decide for themselves when their lives should end. But until they die, care is still essential: for (major) medical maintenance, but also for pacemakers, replacement hips, cataract operations and so on. Globalization of care will take off. The bulk of such medical care will take place in health centres in Dubai, Thailand, Turkey, Eastern Europe and other low-cost countries. Regular treatment, particularly for the young, will still be concentrated in North-West and Middle Europe.

Financing

People have to be able to finance it all. The expectation is that, during the coming decades, the financing of, and policy regarding financing, the lifestyle of seniors will be the most important matter on the political and social agenda. In all countries the struggle for pensions will erupt, a struggle between generations. Take the UK, where a time bomb is ticking under the pension system. The recent advice of a commission under the leadership of Adair Turner, former chairman of the CBI, a UK employers association, was that this can only be disarmed by decisive and politically controversial measures.

According to this report, 12 million UK citizens (40 per cent of the working population) are saving far too little for their old age. Over the next three decades pensions will drop by an average of 30 per cent if no hard choices are made about raising taxes and national insurance

contributions, obligatory additional saving, and a rise in the retirement age. Turner says that UK citizens have, for many years, imagined that they will live in luxury partly because many pension funds are linked to the stock exchange index. "Irrational behaviour" on the exchange and a "delayed acknowledgement of society becoming greyer" meant that many pension funds only took measures towards the end of the 1990s. That was at least 20 years too late, and the measures are still inadequate, claims Turner.

In Italy, France and Germany the trade unions have protested, often with mass demonstrations, against any rise in the age of retirement. France has a uniform pension system. When the government recently wanted to raise the age of retirement from 55 to 58, it affected everybody. In Italy similar circumstances played a role, but there an additional problem was that people in the private sector had to work longer than their colleagues in the civil service. At the end of last year, the German government lowered the sum that the elderly receive from the state.

Oil-rich Norway will also be confronted with the financial consequences of population ageing. Norwegians have become lazy because of this wealth, analysts claim. It is all to do with the income from the daily Norwegian oil production of 3.3 million barrels, which is deposited into a government investment fund. This recently reached the 1,000 billion kronen (more than €121 billion) mark, which makes it one of the richest pension funds in the world. But the oil fund is not bottomless. The Norwegian central bank, which manages the fund, recently reported that it cannot pay more than a quarter of the Norwegian pension bill. Taxpayers will have to take care of the rest themselves. The Norwegian government has introduced radical reforms to the state pension system, which is now 37 years old. It is considering raising the pension age from 62 to 67. At the same time, Oslo will cap the annual growth in state pensions.

Most European countries have set aside too little for pensions. An exception here is the Netherlands, with a saving fund of more than €500 billion. Despite the most serious stock exchange crash since 1929 which hit the country recently, this piggy bank is larger than the annual production of goods and services in the Netherlands.

In 2004 the European Commission published a report *Unequal Welfare States: Distributive Consequences of Population Ageing in Six European Countries,* which shows that ageing and decline in the population have led to larger differences in the welfare state in six European countries. The report concludes:

- In almost all European countries, the population is ageing. Since pensioners in general have less income than those working, income inequality will show a slight increase over the next 25 years. Poverty will also increase slightly in most countries.
- If, from 2010, all EU countries meet the employment aims laid down in the Lisbon agreement, both income inequality and poverty will increase less than they would otherwise. In France and Italy, such an increase in employment participation will actually result in a decrease in these areas.
- A policy of lowering pensions will be beneficial to the financing of social welfare, but will increase income inequality and poverty.
- If, in coming years, countries wish to introduce measures to make it possible to fund social welfare and at the same time restrict the effects on income inequality and poverty, then the "Scandinavian model" seems the best choice. Higher employment participation is central to this model.

(Source: www.scp.nl)

Virtually all countries in Europe are facing growing costs for social welfare and private pensions. The ability to finance this can be improved by getting more people to work, for example by letting people work to an older age or by stimulating women to participate in the work process. In the participation scenario, it is thus assumed that by 2010 all countries will satisfy the employment agreements reached in Lisbon in 2000. The aim is to have 50 per cent of people between the ages of 55 and 64, 60 per cent of women, and 70 per cent of the total population in work. When more people continue working to a higher age, they will build up more rights and their pension will be higher. Such a policy can reduce income inequality and curb an increase in poverty.

Another possibility is a decrease in pensions. This policy has positive effects on the financing of the social welfare system, but negative consequences for both income inequality and poverty. If the elderly receive a lower pension it will bring them closer to the poverty level.

An analysis of the characteristics of existing European systems reveals five types of welfare state. The Scandinavian countries have, in general, a social security structure that is largely aimed at increasing labour participation: virtually all women work full-time and the pension age is relatively high. The Anglo-Saxon countries (the United Kingdom and Ireland) have a system in which benefits are restricted to combating the worst forms of poverty. In several of the new EU member states (Poland, Hungary, the Czech Republic and Slovakia) the benefits system is fairly restricted. The Mediterranean countries (Italy, Spain, Portugal and Greece) enjoy a fairly generous pension system, but benefits to non-pensioners are still rather limited. The Continental countries (Germany, France, Austria, Belgium and Luxemburg) have, on the whole, good regulations for employees. Many of these regulations are based on the cost-winner model and stimulate early retirement (source: www.scp.nl).

Conclusion

Until recently, the European population was predominantly white. Today, it is strongly multi-ethnic. Immigration during the last decades, zebra marriages, and the arrival of all sorts of tourists have all contributed to this. But there is decreasing support for immigration, and Fort Europe has become a fact.

At the same time, the population is ageing and the total number of Europeans is shrinking. That has consequences for the density of the population. An increasing number of ugly and uneconomical cities will be demolished in the near future. In their place will be nature reserves, or there will be facilities for the new European economic foundations, such as recreation. The new or renovated buildings will be historical, or will be replicas of traditional regional architecture. The depopulated rural areas will once again be populated, but now by part-time seniors and juniors, who wish to enjoy the pleasures of both town and country. Since the new inhabitants will largely be from the cities, there will be an increasing urbanization of rural culture.

Non-Europeans from Asian countries that are becoming more prosperous will purchase their rural retreats in picturesque parts of the European countryside. This will lead to greater industry in the countryside. Busloads of seniors and Asian tourists will come to see how things work in this "human zoo". The migration will largely be from West to East. This will largely be due to medical care tourism and the fact that real estate is cheaper in the east. A fear of further Islamization in Western Europe will also play a role. (For more about this, see Megatrend 7.) The lifestyles and the way people fill their days will change too. Management of boredom will become an important economic pillar: maintaining a virtual "family feeling" and "regional feeling" and cultivating contacts with extended families will be important activities. In short: living with fewer people will, in 15 to 45 years' time, result in a lifestyle that is different from the one we currently know.

Megatrend **2**
The new tribalization

Introduction

Europe still has a strong attraction to people from all over the world. Gays from around the world come to Berlin, Paris, Barcelona, London, Cologne and Amsterdam. Inhabitants of previous European colonies move to their former colonizer: the Congolese to Belgium, Africans and Vietnamese to France and Belgium, Surinamese and Indonesians to the Netherlands, Indians and Pakistanis to the UK. In addition, various diasporas exist in Europe: Jews can be found in all European countries, and so too can Chinese. A large Turkish diaspora can be found in many European countries, such as Germany and the Netherlands. Muslims are present in virtually every European country, although there are fewer in the East. Gypsies (Romanies) live in various places spread over the whole of Europe.

Seniors are also on the move. An increasing number of European seniors choose to live, full-time or part-time, in other places, regions or countries. Sometimes it is an individual choice, but often they live in groups. The number of over-65s who enjoy their old age in Eastern Europe is increasing. Houses there are (still) cheap and the cost of living is three to five times lower than in the West. But the most *pensionados* still live in France, Spain and Portugal. Three months a year, Benidorm is populated by young people; for the rest of the year it is literally grey. There is even a stretch of sand there that is covered with a wooden deck so that people in wheelchairs can enjoy the sea air. For those who wish to venture further onto the beach, there are wheelchairs with large yellow plastic tyres. Broad and without profile, they are perfect for pushing an adult through the sand. The terraces, too, offer walking sticks, rolling pathways and other help attributes. Yet strangely enough, it doesn't seem out of place. Life on the boulevard is far from dull. Every morning gym lessons are held at various places on the beach, one of them taught by an 80-year-old. Anybody who wants to can join in. People jump up and down on the balconies with a view of the sea. There is live music in a number of bars. Old men in smart white suits sing Frank Sinatra and Bing Crosby standards, accompanied by a tape or synthesizer. If a band is performing and the music is infectious, people dance. People chatter and flirt, admire and show off. It is grey happiness.

Benidorm, famous for its white sands, has long been a place for people spending the winter, largely British and Dutch with a limited budget. It proves that the democratization of the elderly works: not only are the more affluent European elderly able to enjoy part-time living in two places, so are those with lower incomes, and in the near future this phenomenon will only increase, with Turkey becoming a popular destination. The Turks have already built a replica of Amsterdam, especially for these target groups.

Not a "melting pot" but a "salad bowl"

Tribes have come into being throughout Europe – groups of people who share a culture, religion or lifestyle, who have spread

far afield yet feel a strong cohesion. Europe has, in fact, become an enormous salad bowl inhabited by large groups of people, dressed with a European sauce. In this century, the number of tribes will increase and the size of most tribes will also grow. The tribes manifest themselves increasingly as simultaneous partners and rivals. Sometimes they work together, if their interests demand this. In other cases they are (economic and/or political) opponents. The characteristic that distinguishes these tribes from "mainstream Europe" is that they live in several places. They are people who live part-time in their homeland and part-time elsewhere. They are world citizens, continentals, new Europeans, who really do not need a homeland.

In this way, the distinctive experiences and lifestyles of traditional nation-states disappear. The various nation-states in Europe continue to exist and retain their importance as government-legal entities.

There are an increasing number of economic, financial and political cooperative agreements. That is logical in an integration process. But it is unlikely that national governments will allow themselves in the future to be degraded into vassals of a powerful European government, as happened, for example, in the United States. There, although the individual states retain control of a number of important functions (every US state, for example, decides how best to organize its welfare system), government is dominated by the Federal administration, which has powers laid down in the US Constitution that are far greater than those of the European Union.

It is naturally unavoidable that in Europe too, central authority will grow stronger in the coming decades. Although the 2005 rejection of the draft European constitution by France and the Netherlands offers little hope that this will now be adopted, the influence of the European Commission and the European Parliament should increase as time passes. A European head of state is also a possibility. He or she is unlikely to have as much power as the president of China or the United States, but in any case would have an important symbolic function. A charismatic, multilingual European president, whose prime function is to act as an ambassador, can help establish European integration firmly in the hearts of both mainstream Europeans and the tribes.

"Glocalization"

Increasing European unification, as evidenced in the euro, pan-European law-making, and the disappearance of borders and import duties, is perceived by the European population on the one hand as easy and comfortable, but on the other as increasing anonymity and alienation. As the importance of Europe increases and globalization continues, many fall back on regionalism. To ensure that the European feeling will be maintained, there will be an increase of regionalism. People will cultivate their regional identities and invest in them, learn regional languages better, and acquaint themselves better with the history and culture of their local area, even if they were not born there. Regionalism will rise above borders. In some areas it has existed for some time but has now been given a new impulse. In others it is totally new. Think about the Basques (France/Spain), the Catalans (Spain), the Frisians (the Netherlands), the Flemish and the Walloons (Belgium), the Lapps (Scandinavia), the East Frisians (Germany), the Kurds (Turkey, Syria, Iran and Iraq), and the Laz (Turkey).

Pure nationalism will, in the new Europe, become a thing of the past, since it disturbs bicultural thinking and acting, it disturbs the ability to entertain more loyalties simultaneously, and it disturbs the distance between the nation-state and the region, all of which are vital factors for success in the new era. And yet nationalism will not disappear completely. It has assumed a different form that can be typified as "glocalization". Alongside the (European) globalization that is embraced, there is

a revaluation of local, regional, personal identity. In practice, these two can go perfectly hand in hand. You act as a globalist, you feel yourself a nationalist or a regionalist: the attitude of the future. Ultimately, we are all world citizens.

What makes tribes so attractive is that tribes form networks. Tribe members in all parts of the world are connected to each other and put business each other's way. Thus they form an economy that is separate from any nation state. Chinese and Indians create high GDPs outside their home countries. In the past, the Jews and Armenians did this too, and now the idea seems to be taking root throughout the world: tribalization is taken on major dimensions. This megatrend will have consequences for Europe in a whole range of areas.

Different people, different wishes

Every tribe has its preferred way of living, and this gives rise to new trends. For example, there is something that could be called "Floridaization". This phenomenon, named for the migration of American seniors to the state of Florida, means that people want to go somewhere else when they retire, preferably somewhere that is warm and pleasant, where there are good facilities, and where they can enjoy themselves. Because of the ageing throughout Europe, an increasing number of people will be going into retirement. This is certainly not unexpected. The European baby-boomers, people who were born soon after the Second World War, are approaching the age of retirement. They are generally well educated, have had good jobs, have money, and are healthy. What's more, they are adventurous and are certainly not aiming to spend the rest of their lives tending window-boxes. They can be called YEEPIEs: Young Energetic Elderly People Into Everything. Although members of this tribe will retain their roots in their homelands, they will increasingly spend long or short periods abroad. Seniors from North-West Europe will settle en masse in Europe's Sunbelt: southern France, Spain, Portugal, but also farther afield in Thailand, Uruguay, Argentina and South Africa.

These seniors are creating a trend that is also being followed by young people: part-time living. This is matched with a lifestyle that we could call five-star living. We have become accustomed to this, partly through holidays in cheap countries such as Turkey. Five-star living means luxurious living in an urban environment, in a security-protected apartment in the middle of things, near to shops and facilities. This is combined with a house in the countryside where people can enjoy rural life and tend their gardens, giving them the best of both worlds simultaneously. Part-time living and five-star living are also available in your own country or region: you have an apartment in Berlin and, for example, a country house near the Polish border.

Luxury apartments in cities or other places are increasingly exploited by five-star hotel chains. You live in the centre of Vienna or Paris in a Hilton apartment. You have your own apartment in a luxurious, safe complex in the centre of town. The Hilton personnel can, if you want, provide room service, and you can make use of the hotel facilities such as a swimming pool and exercise area. Doing the shopping will also change: anybody who lives in two different places will no longer do the weekly shopping on Saturday. Thanks to this, there is a market for multinational supermarket chains that can carefully monitor the border-hopping consumers with the latest customer relationship management (CRM) methods. Example: you are citizen X who spends eight months of the year in Cologne and four months on Majorca. You will appreciate a supermarket with branches in Cologne and Majorca that offer an assortment of products to match your lifestyle and your needs in this period of your life. Such a supermarket can supply these needs since it can monitor the target group. It can streamline its purchasing, and be efficient, effective and profitable.

At the same time, there is a market for local shops, as long as there is a large enough supply of consumers. It's nice if you can buy local bread, local jam and local ingredients in Majorca. In the framework of the experience economy, you enjoy two totally different experiences in one year. In Majorca you live as a (German-speaking) Spaniard in the countryside; in Cologne you live as a busy town-dweller who consumes German urban products. The expectation is that in areas that are more densely populated and where it pays marketing-wise, there will be more local immigrant facilities, shops and products, while in "emptier" areas there will be more pan-European supermarkets.

In all cities, neighbourhoods will grow where tribe members live together, following the American example. Cities will have a China-town, a Little Moscow, a Little Rio, a Little India, a gay neighbourhood and an older people's neighbourhood. An ever-increasing number of languages will be spoken, even in those areas where traditionally only one language was spoken. In Provence you will hear more German and English, just as you will in various Italian rural areas.

Estate agents that sell property in new EU countries such as the Czech Republic and Hungary will do a roaring trade. In a Dutch newspaper I read about Bas van Schelt (66) and his wife Margo (52) who left the Netherlands for Hungary in 2004. Their new home is in Tiszaders, approximately 160 kilometres to the east of Budapest. It is

a beautiful area, close to the enormous Hortobagy Puszta national park. They have been coming here for years, having purchased a holiday house here ten years ago. Friends who live down the road bought a gigantic house here four years ago for just 20,000. You don't have to be rich to buy a property here, but the prices are starting to rise. There are a growing number of Germans in the area and it is becoming more and more popular. This migration to the East will increase in the coming decades. More and more seniors from the Western part of Europe will move to the Eastern part, which will give the area an economic boost.

Despite the problems with pensions and the fact that people will have to work to an older age in various European countries, demographers expect that grey emigration will persist. More and more

seniors have purchased a second home before they reach retirement age, and once they stop working they will move there for good. And as so often happens, the first to do so will act as an example that many others will follow. The growth of "two-pension households", where both partners enjoy a pension, will ensure that there is enough money to undertake such a step.

As seniors spend more time abroad, there will need to be good travel facilities. After all, they will want to see their children, grandchildren and other family and friends with a certain regularity. They will, of course, maintain virtual friendships via the Internet, webcam, and an increasingly cheaper telephone (including telephony via the Internet). It is unthinkable that budget airlines will disappear from the air for some time to come.

Intersections

Because people want to live in several places simultaneously, and transport between places becomes much more important when they commute rather than just visit a holiday home once a year, new intersections will arise in the infrastructure. The areas around train stations will become important residential intersections for people who live part-time in the city and part-time in the country, but these will also become important places for pieds-à-terre. Stations that serve high-speed trains will in particular become new urban intersections; for those who live there, travel to their country house in some other European country becomes a lot less complicated. Changes will arise in logistics and transport. The phenomenon of the coach trip has a healthy future, and there will be more opportunity for various taxi concepts, car-sharing, car rentals and so on. The European roads will not become less crowded, because the many tourists who come here will also need to get around. And city trips, short holiday breaks, day trips and so on for a group of bored fit seniors, and the fact that we will work less and have more spare time, will mean that the roads will be as busy as ever.

Building

In the future, buildings will become increasingly concentrated. We shall live closer together, even though we shall have more space thanks to the decline in the European population. For those who live in the city, this will imply that they live close together in dwellings that are built on top of each other. They will be safe, with many facilities and a large number of shops. Despite the fact that we shall shop more on the Internet, physical shopping will remain an experience that we would not like to do without, if only because it provides an opportunity for showing ourselves off, looking at people and being admired. There will also be a lot of entertainment in urban concentrations. People want to have fun, and want it in all shapes and sizes. Concerts, shows, museums, temporary exhibitions, sing-songs, spiritual meetings, revues, cabarets, stand-up comedy, theatre, real-life soaps – you name it. The city becomes the backdrop for people's lives. This life takes place largely in the old city centres and the nearby areas. These will be renovated in the coming period (if they have become rundown). The lower classes that now live there will leave the area, whether voluntarily or under pressure. Empty areas in city centres (such as the City of London and the centre of Brussels) will have new life breathed into them, and a greater return will be achieved from the expensive ground.

Architecture and globalization

Albert Vidal

Of all the activities that humanity has developed throughout history, architecture is in my opinion the one that gives the best and most complete view of reality. I say this, of course, from my position as an architect, and thus from the basis of all the knowledge that has formed me. Undoubtedly other people could make similar proposals concerning their own area of expertise, but this is not the place for such a discussion.

Everything that is built is an architectural expression of culture; people should not immediately wish to make a value judgement on whether it is beautiful or good. From here we can see in architecture the value of the combination of a creative mind – and artistic and philosophical heritage – economic industry, social activity and technological development. The balance between these various elements can help us discover whether a building is good or not.

In general – and still from the point of view of everything that has been built – we discover, until the beginning of the modernistic movement, a close relationship between location and architecture. We could go further: the expansion of the classic empires (Greece, Rome) and the more recent empires (those of the United Kingdom, Spain, the Netherlands, Germany) and the extensive migration that this brought about, it is true, in the architecture of the homeland being reproduced in the conquered areas, for both houses and more symbolic buildings, but the building style also adapted itself to the location. In some cases, this created an aesthetic and technological symbiosis with remarkable results, such as the Dutch building style and its application in Indonesia.

Since the arrival of modernism, a new situation has emerged. The expansion of the fundamentals of modernism and the technology that allows it to develop have resulted in architecture that is similar wherever you go. The same patterns are applied everywhere in the world. Whether a building is in Moscow, Paris or Cape Town, one encounters extremely uniform solutions.

Only in concrete cases by exceptional builders (such as Alvar Aalto or Alvaro Siza) is the theory of modernism successfully expressed, and this raises their work to masterpieces. One of the fundamentals of this expression is the relationship that the buildings have with their location, in every possible perspective. Siza also involves the political circumstances under which his work is achieved.

The process of globalization in which we are immersed means (in many cases) a step forward. On the other hand, however, globalization ignores not only the characteristics of the location, but also those of the culture, economy or production forces of the places it enters. In its constant attempts to find consumers and attract their attention, it reacts exclusively to commercial considerations or image.

Certainly, globalization forces many European architects to extend their working arena to far from their own homes, in China, the Middle East or some other place in the world. Nevertheless, it is quite clear that their architectonic production would result in a higher quality and improved understanding (and thus greater appreciation) if they adhered more strongly to the local culture, economy and technology.

This leads me to believe, I repeat, that architecture is a tool that can build bridges – both literally and figuratively – between various societies and cultures, and thus enrich the heritage of humanity.

Albert Vidal (Spain) is an architect.

Ageing and the future of package design

Ageing in Europe creates major changes in package design. We shall see less pastel colours being used in the package designs of food and other articles in supermarkets. The eyesight of older consumers makes clearer colour schemes necessary, as a recent survey of the Dutch companies Dexter and Newcom Research & Consultancy shows. Bottles, cans and packages for food should be designed in new ways, in order to enable people to open them with less muscle power. The survey of Dexter and Newcom Research & Consultancy shows a hit list of items that older consumers use to open bottles, cans and other packages: a pair of pincers, a screwdriver and a pair of scissors. Teeth are not used any more to open packages containing snacks.

Conclusion

Europe will become a real "salad bowl", and that is good. Everybody will come into contact with more and more other cultures and other lifestyles, and this will promote the integration of Europe. Of course this will have consequences for local and regional cultural expressions. To prevent these disappearing altogether, people will increasingly go in search of their identity. The continuing existence of separate cultures, customs and lifestyles will thus be safeguarded.

We shall live everywhere and nowhere, and thus take our needs with us wherever we go, and this will have consequences for day-to-day matters such as housing, shopping, logistics, medical care and financing. The smart business person can profit from this and try to satisfy the various needs. The inhabitants of the salad bowl called Europe will be an interesting market.

Megatrend **3**
From traditions to technological, spiritual, and environmental revolutions

Introduction

Europe is in a transitional period in which three major developments will radically change the face of the traditional "good old mother Europe". Technology, spirituality and the environment will change so drastically that they will totally reshape our lives. In the West of Europe over the past decades we have become spoiled by peace and an unprecedented prosperity. In the East of Europe that is not the case, and the Balkans, in particular, have been plagued by disturbances. New times have arrived, however, and technology will play a major role in this. The superficial structure of life in the 21st century in Europe will change; the underlying structure will, however, remain largely the same. Happiness is, apparently, something that can to a certain degree be manufactured: but people have to make the right choices. Many traditions will disappear in the new Europe: new technology inventions will cause our lifestyles to change, and the time we spend on housekeeping, for example, will decrease. It will not go completely: new inventions will also introduce new and different work. The arrival of email has given us a new time-consuming task – reading and answering emails, and doing it quickly, because people who send the emails expect a prompt answer.

We shall need help in managing all this technological paraphernalia, and religion and spirituality will be re-evaluated. Every person feels the need for *mythos* and *logos*. Now technology itself will have a mythical function. In industrial and post-industrial societies, technology induces the same mixture of admiration, wariness and awe that people of old felt for natural phenomena such as thunder and storms, and for the religious implications of these.

The climate will still be subject to change, caused not so much by the greenhouse effect that so many in Europe allow to blind them, but by changes taking place in the sun itself. These are changes that take place naturally from time to time; insignificant human beings can do nothing to alter that, either positively or negatively. Climate changes will give Europe in the 21st century a new face. Rivers will regularly breach their banks; there will need to be flood areas created for the water that suddenly rises in the main rivers, such as the Rhine. The sea level will rise, while some areas of Europe will sink, as is currently happening in Venice. A new form of water management will be essential. Fresh water will become scarcer, the sea will be used more intensively (more food can be harvested from the sea, such as seaweed), and there will also be new ways of generating energy.

It will certainly become warmer in Europe, and at the same time wetter. This means that in non-Latin parts of Europe, lifestyles and cultures will become more Latin, like the traditional culture of Southern Europe: more outside living, more terraces, more "promenading" (and people taking better care of themselves, their clothing and appearance) – although always under the protecting eye of security cameras, and even personal bodyguards. The wellness industry (and better medical care) will grow drastically, elderly people will look younger, and old Europe will be given a new lease of life thanks to technology, spirituality and a different climate.

Technological revolution: the miracles of technique

Technology has always brought drastic changes to our lives. The introduction of electricity, the light bulb, radio, television, fax, computers, aircraft, cars, photos and film changed our lifestyles and the way we spent our days. This technological revolution is still in full swing. In fact, the major technological inventions that will radically change our lives in the first half of the 21st century already exist. Sony, Siemens, Nokia, Philips and other technology giants have already applied for patents for various important inventions, as have freelance inventors.

Digitalization is now getting under way in Eastern Europe; thanks to the lower wages (in comparison with those in Western Europe), it can be realized a lot quicker there. Here are some examples of what lies in wait for us in the field of technology.

Much is expected of the so-called RFID-chip. This is a chip the size of a grain of sand that can couple various processes and place them in a chain. For example: your car has a malfunction. Its computer becomes aware of this and contacts the garage or the rescue service. It then shows you the way to the garage and orders a taxi to take you home.

Our housekeeping will soon be under the spell of domotica (ICT applications in the home) and will soon be managed by home computers. They will track whether we have sufficient food, household articles and such things, and get in touch with the nearest supermarket if that is not the case. Outside our homes we will have a delivery box where the delivery person from the supermarket can leave products, with a cooled section for perishables. Our home computer will know our daily rhythm and adjust various tasks in the house to match it. Do you always wake up at 8 o'clock and start your day with a fresh espresso? The home computer will control the espresso machine so that the smell of fresh coffee greets you when you get out of bed. If you are arriving home later than planned, you simply send an sms to the computer and it will heat up your food later. These systems will be user-friendly, with only a few buttons instead of dozens of complicated functions and thick user manuals. Partly because of the demands of the growing senior market, technology will be applied to ensure that the equipment in the house is much simpler to use.

All sorts of inventions that are already technically possible, such as the self-thinking vacuum-cleaner and the self-thinking lawn mower, will gradually enter our homes. The integration of audio, television and computer is nearly here. The retractable flex-screen already exists. It is a sheet of plastic, the size of a tabloid, which can be rolled up, folded up, and viewed anywhere, at home on the sofa, in the train or in a park. You can download anything to it, from newspaper or magazine to a book. You either take out a subscription or order a single copy, and there you are: the pages of *The Times*, or the newest issue of *Fortune* or *Time*. If an article particularly interests you, you mark it and save it. It means less work for the already scarce newspaper delivery kids, and less work for newspaper kiosks and printers, but a very large market for content providers.

In the not too distant future, nuclear energy combined with hydrogen energy will be used as an alternative to oil and gas. Technically it is already possible, but the risks are large. A terrorist attack on a nuclear power station, for example, would be a humanitarian and environmental disaster. What's more, oil is comparatively speaking still cheaper. And yet China is already demanding more and more oil, and in the future, certainly if the unrest in the Middle East continues, this alternative source of energy could replace oil sooner than we think. The price of oil will then be so high that we shall be prepared to accept the risks involved in nuclear energy.

The arrival of DNA computers (computers that, just like living creatures, have their own DNA) has already been announced, and so too have quantum computers, which will achieve what is called "singularity" by 2020. This means that chips can do just as much as the human brain. The consequences of this irreversible process are staggering. Ian Pearson thinks that, thanks to the large, collective, autonomous power of the computer chip, human life will come to a standstill by 2085. The use of robots will increase dramatically. In June 2004, the eighth "Global Football Championship for Robots" was held – the RoboCup 2004 in Lisbon. More than 1600 participants from 37 countries participated in the matches, which were held between footballing robots which operated themselves. The first match between football robots and the winners of the Championship League is expected by 2050.

In the food sector, Ray Kurzweil expects that the production of nano-food will be a fact by 2049. This food, which has the same taste and nutritional content as organic food, is cheap and readily available. By then we shall be familiar with *functional food*, a method that allows consumers to eat food that better reflects their nutritional needs. Work is also taking place on food delivery systems that allow tastes to be released at the right moment during the meal, and on lab-on-a-chip technology to safeguard food during the production process.

Much is expected of genetically modified (GM) food. There is a battle under way for the legal acceptance of this type of food, but it seems that this is a rearguard action. Consumers are currently critical, because the advantages are not clear to them, and their protests are largely directed at the increasing power of certain manufacturers. If GM foods show clear advantages over non-GM products and there are no major catastrophes, the protests will gradually ebb away. Already 70 per cent of all cotton and soya and 35 per cent of all grain produced in the United States is genetically modified. In Israel, Turkey and the United States, experiments are being held with coloured cotton, which will allow naturally coloured products to be introduced onto the market. The second green revolution in the agro-industry is about to break out. This is also expected to result in a decrease in the prices of agricultural products rather than an increase.

In the medical care sector, a large number of developments attract attention. Important applications in stem-cell technology are expected, including the replacement of heart muscle cells that are no longer functional. Considerable research is also taking place into possibilities for new nerve cells for Parkinson's and Alzheimer's patients and for paraplegics, as well as new skin for burn patients. It obviously appeals to the imagination that human tissue and even organs should be able to be replaced by substitutes grown from stem cells harvested from the body. Discovering this omnipotent stem cell is referred to as finding the Holy Grail of biology. Some expect that this will cause a fundamental change in the field of surgery.

Developments also showing promise include replacing sensory organs such as the light-sensitive tissue in the eye and the cilium in the ear with microelectronic mechanical systems (MEMS). This means integration between the nerve cells in the human body and advanced microelectronics. Here again, applications for paraplegics are also being developed. And an implanted chip can automatically handle the required dosage of medicine (creating so-called smart pills).

Futurologist Wim de Ridder argues that it is certain that communication between people will develop rapidly:

> Our opinions about this are constantly adapting themselves. The chance is great that Big Brother is not the nightmare described by George Orwell, but will be seen as a welcome development. The cameras that are now seen everywhere give us a sense of security that we are members of a collective that – for whatever reason – is interested in us. The robot will also find a place in this world. If we want, robots are friendlier than people.

The future of the Internet

In 2005 the Internet celebrated its 35th anniversary. It has brought Europe many blessings: email, chat, websites, e-news, you name it. But every advantage has its disadvantage, and that is true of the Internet. The enormous damage that has been caused worldwide by hackers and cyber criminals with viruses, extortion and fraud is nothing compared with what computer users can expect in the future. During the last few years attacks with armies of tens of thousands of computers, the so-called botnets, have become all too common. In 2004 there was a botnet of one million computers: one million hacked PCs that were all like zombies under the control of one single person! The chance that an arbitrary computer will be used remotely for an attack on the Internet will be greater in the future than it is now.

Marcus Sachs, director of the American SANS Internet Storm Center, which tracks down like a cyber-meteorologist storms on the Internet, thinks that Internet at the start of the 21st century is a mess:

> I would dare to state that almost every computer with an Internet connection is confronted with an infection, whether successful or not. Every week we encounter new digital zombie armies, the one more ingenious than the other. They are used for espionage. Or they smother companies by visiting websites en masse and bombarding companies with emails, sometimes for extortion. A company that does not pay up is simply shut down.

Alternatively the netbots send emails that look like official bank correspondence. Those who reply and give away their banking details can expect their bank account to be plundered. The user of the computer often has no idea at all that the computer has been taken over by criminals: it generally happens at night, when the owner is in bed.

Terrorism

New technology will also fall into the hands of terrorists. It is no longer the threat that is emitted by nations that dominates our thinking – with some exceptions – but the threat from groups that represent no formal power. De Ridder says:

> The power of such groups is so great because the means at their disposal allow them to unleash wide-spread terror. It is almost impossible to prevent the threat of anthrax. In

addition, the assumption is justified that genetic technology that is developed for commercial use can also be used to kill plants, animals and people. The fear is largely due to the knowledge that the raw materials for this are readily available. A laboratory can be fitted out using equipment that does not cost more than US$10,000. Thousands of students throughout the world have worked with such equipment and materials. There is also a fear that, should certain viruses be used by terrorists, it will be impossible to eradicate them from the environment.

Attention is also being given to recombinant DNA designer weapons which can be used selectively. Weapons can be developed that only attack specific ethnic groups, or that affect the mood and behaviour of people. It is hardly surprising, then, that the fear of chemical weapons is so great. In 2003, the most-read book in the world of futurology was a study by Martin Rees published under the title *Our Final Century*. His conclusion is that the chance of our civilization surviving until the end of the current century is no larger than 50 per cent. In short, the technology of the 21st century can, whether or not by accident, seriously threaten life and bring it to a premature end.

New technology, new lifestyles

During the last century, technology created a new economy: the agricultural economy became an industrial economy. Now Europe is becoming a service economy. The lifestyles connected with the economy also change. Within a century the lifestyle of a farmer became totally different, and the number of farmers also decreased and new professional groups emerged, with their own new lifestyles. There was, for example, the group of factory workers, with a radically different lifestyle from that of the farmer.

Industrialization of the agricultural industry resulted in greater yields: various European nations (France, the Netherlands) became the world's largest agricultural nations, largely as a result of the productivity that was thus achieved.

As we have said: technology changes our lives and our lifestyles. Sixty years ago, my grandmother from India had a full-time job looking after the housekeeping: maintaining the latrine (the predecessor to the water closet) took a lot of time, as did cooking on wood and coal before the arrival of the gas and electric cooker, the provision of fresh meat before the arrival of refrigerator and freezer, cleaning the house before the introduction of the vacuum cleaner, and doing shopping by horse and cart instead of car or scooter.

Technology more than anything else made women's emancipation possible, in my opinion. If men had had to take over the work of women in housekeeping, and it required as much energy now as it did 60 years ago, women's emancipation would never have come

about. Of course it is possible to add a certain nuance here. Technological and social changes are inextricably intertwined. Before households were electrified, the houses of the averagely well-off had stone or wood floors, with mats that needed to be beaten several times a year. The vacuum cleaner was not particularly well suited to this, and so fitted carpeting was introduced. The new wall-to-wall carpeting, women's magazines announced, had to be vacuumed at least once a week. Beating mats was physically demanding, and men generally helped. But the vacuum cleaner, at least in the first decades of its existence, was used almost entirely by women. This example illustrates that the career of a new technology can never be seen in isolation. Most changes are not anticipated, and their effects are often contradictory to what their inventors intended, as is shown by Edward Tenner in his hilarious book *Why Things Bite Back* (1996). But that's neither here nor there.

Email and other technical inventions make it easier than ever before to work from home. The trend is for large work organizations to grow smaller, so the workers of the near future are more likely to work in smaller organizations. Employers will find that it is more manageable and less trouble to work in networked organizations and with "collective entrepreneurial responsibility" than to work with flocks of salaried people. The first of such collectives will be in the medical care sector: collectives of nursing staff, for example, or of house-care nurses.

Busyness

The way we spend our days is clearly influenced by the technological revolution. We sleep for fewer hours, because there is now a lot of experience after sunset. A century ago we slept for 12 hours a night, now we sleep for eight. In a century's time, this is likely to have dropped to six hours a night. Other lifestyles, all sorts of meditation, healthier food, supplemented with vitamin pills and other

energy boosters, will give us the energy that we used to derive from sleep. We seem to be heading for the "end of sleep". All those hours that we are awake each day need to be used or filled in ways that make life worthwhile. We have to be able to use all this increasing amount of human energy somewhere. We have to keep busy, be entertained. The youth channel MTV maintains that young people are able to do several things at the same time: watch television and at the same time talk on the phone or send an sms, read and answer emails on the computer, and hold a conversation with people in the same room. A spokesperson for MTV commented, "It is quite possible that research will show that the brains of young people have been changed by this 'multiple brain usage'."

The European research agency Motivaction has published research findings on the way we fill our days. These show a number of changing needs and motives which explain and signal new trends. "Not wanting to miss anything" has led to "de-hasting". People are in search of a good combination of work, care tasks and free time. This arises partly from the phenomenon of being "threatened by time stress": increasingly, we have the feeling that we are under time pressure. That is why we deal with time more rationally and in a more planned manner than ever before. This is also connected to a "decreasing identification with work". Growing prosperity gives us the feeling that work is making too many demands on our private lives. Our striving for economic and material status and the urge to move up socially are decreasing, according to the research. A result of this is the trend of "nostalgia for domesticity". People indicate a new desire for the security of the home environment. We prefer to stay at home with friends rather than go out. Staying at home in your spare time is becoming more appealing. The home will once again become an oasis of rest in our hectic and complex society.

"Cocooning" is on the increase, largely as a result of our feelings of insecurity (see Megatrend 5). We therefore want more entertainment in the home. That is easy enough, because television, audio and the

Internet will soon be integrated, and that will allow the home entertainment industry to grow dramatically. We shall soon have various flat screens in the home, in different places, where we can view almost anything. Space will be put to different uses. We won't have to waste metres of shelf space on CDs; instead we shall have one small, compact carrier where we have saved hundreds if not thousands of hours of music. Artists will bring out their new repertoire via the Internet, and customers will pay to download it track by track. There will be no more music stores. Equipment will become increasingly invisible, while until now visibility has been very important. People will no longer be able to boast about their expensive audio equipment from brand X, or their television from brand Y: the technology of the future will wear a burka. At the same time, old traditional board games such as Monopoly will regain their popularity, together with digital games for children and adults. Web-shopping will increase but not replace real shopping, for that is a form of entertainment that will remain. There will be an increasing integration of web-shopping and live shopping, for example with people ordering goods via the Internet and collecting them from local shops.

The entertainment industry also beckons outside the home, although it will be increasingly heavily guarded because of terrorism. People watch films at home, but there are some films they prefer to watch in a cinema. Theatre, opera, musicals: the market for these will grow explosively, just as it will for live concerts and the like. There will be more integration of theatre and dinner, as is found in the Berlin revues, and more tea dances and other forms of dancing at senior-friendly times – those who are past 40 no longer go to a disco at one in the morning.

Education, healthcare, and wellness

The education system of the future is already on the drawing-board. Children and students will attend school part-time, and take on the care of older people part-time. That implies that people will leave school and graduate later (at least, later than we have been accustomed to until now) than in those countries with a more balanced population. School will become a more integrated part of the lifestyle. The extended school day will be normal. It will be regarded as handy and normal to integrate school and homes for the elderly in the same building, or in any case close to each other.

In these times of haste and new technologies, people will place increasing value on wellness. The word "wellness" is already used in German and other languages. It covers a mixture of welfare, well-being, personal care, relaxation, loss of haste, and is virtually always coupled with water. Wellness centres are virtually always located in spas and other health centres with water, with swimming pools, mud baths, physiotherapy, fitness, saunas, solaria, detoxification and other cures. "Relaxation" is the key thing. Wellness, in its strictest sense, is a way of managing stress. Wellness is one of the main pillars of our lives in the 21st century. Seniors in particular, with a lot of spare time and money, and the need to spend their lives pleasantly with a minimum of stress and a maximum of relaxation, see much in wellness. Spas, thermal baths and other public facilities for wellness have a good future in this market.

People will integrate wellness into their daily lives, in luxury bathrooms with all sorts of extra facilities to help them relax, such as baths, bubble baths, massaging shower-heads, mini-sauna and solaria. In addition, they will regularly visit masseurs, physiotherapists (either specialized or general), beauty specialists and tanning studios. We want to exercise more – something that is essential because we are becoming fatter thanks to our sedentary lifestyle. Children today are heavier than they were in the past, because of the time they spend sitting behind PCs and in front of the television, which has replaced running around and playing.

More sport and more exercise will become an important factor of the wellness trend, even though plastic surgeons will frequently be consulted for weight reduction. Liposuction, liposculpture, and other forms of fat removal by medical specialists will be used increasingly to take care of excess fat.

At the same time, people will want greater contact with nature. We have lost this because of all the hi-tech influences in our lives. They will garden more and visit natural sites. Eco-tourism is in; people will take more walks through forests and along beaches. Nature reserves in the countryside, woods, lakes, beaches, will have good times ahead – as long as they are made accessible for the people of the near future.

Hi-tech healthcare

Hi-tech specialist Jan de Jeu characterized the healthcare of the future as "High tech, high touch". The most remarkable general social development at the moment is, according to him, the incredibly fast growth of computer technology: a spectacular growth in the memory and processing capacity of chips, rapidly diminishing prices, and further miniaturization:

> Every three years, the memory capacity of chips quadruples and the performance of microprocessors increases by a factor of four to five. It is expected that by 2011, one single chip could contain as much information as more than a thousand volumes of the *Encyclopaedia Britannica*. And the game computer that Sega introduced in 1995 contained a chip with more processing power than the Cray supercomputer which, in 1976, was only accessible to top physicists. But it is not only the capacity aspect of the chip revolution that is amazing; the pricing is as well. Take a PC that is supplied by the shop on the corner. The technique inside such a PC contains about 100

million transistors, minute circuits. Yet you can buy it for around 800. And in the coming years, the cost of computing power will drop further. Thanks to miniaturization, the chemist will sees instruments getting smaller and smaller. Pumps, valves, chromatographs – they all now fit on a single chip that can be used to analyse DNA, air or food. What consequences will these developments have for the medical sector? The computer will not only be used for "computing" (data processing, calculations, data storage) but also increasingly for communication and coordination. Thanks to speech recognition we will, in 10 to 15 years, have at our disposal computers that understand everything we say and answer us. Such an interface will allow us to operate equipment, send messages, manage entry and recognition, and request information. Within a few years we will have pocket equipment that combines the power of the traditional supercomputers with video telephony and wireless modems. Everybody will thus be able to have a "personal digital assistant" (PDA).

People will be able to monitor their own health. They will have their PDA that allows them to analyse information about their condition at home. A labchip can perform a blood test at home. The anamneses can, if required, be done interactively every single day. That creates remarkable possibilities for early diagnosis. Preventive measures to avoid further medical complications can be ascertained electronically. Patients can also be referred to a general practitioner or specialist at a much earlier stage. An advantage is that the initial advice is both anonymous and personal.

The work of GPs and specialists will change thanks to this "self-diagnosis". Patients can request the opinion of their doctor via an electronic consultation. And if a visit to the GP or specialist is necessary, the doctor will have a large amount of relevant and up-to-date information about the patient before he or she even arrives at the surgery. Further decentralized diagnosis at the GP or specialist's premises is also possible.

The development of expert systems has even greater consequences for professionals in the medical sector. These are systems that use the history of the patient and his or her test results to provide support during the diagnosis and the development of a treatment plan. Thanks to this support, medical specialists and paramedicals will be able to concentrate more and more on communicative aspects of their profession. Their added value will in the long run probably rely less on their medical-technical knowledge and skills, and more on supporting patients in sickness, recovery, and acceptance of a handicap. This means that communication with patients will take a more central place than it does at the moment.

Patient information will no longer be spread out among different institutions. There will be no more separate files for the hospital, home care or clinic, but one integrated electronic file which, with the authorization of the patient, can be accessed by various parties. The speed of providing information is also increased thanks to this. If a patient goes home to recover under the care of home care specialists and his or her GP, all relevant information will be available to the home-care nurse and GP: prescribed medication, treatment and nursing plan, and appointments for check-ups at the hospital.

Hospitals have a considerable planning problem. Fixing waiting times for an appointment, the planning of consecutive tests, admission and surgery is enormously complex. The logistic problems in a hospital are – at least superficially – comparable to those of a large production company. It is all about throughput times, available production capacity, supply of patients, average downtime and so on. In such companies, including highly complex ones in sectors such as the aviation industry, there are planning systems that allow them to produce "just in time". As soon as similar systems are introduced in the medical sector, it will be possible to plan care processes in a much better and more integrated manner. The GP will be able to make appointments for the patient with the hospital planning system, and the admissions planner will be able to make appointments with home-care and clinic facilities. This will create a "virtual" cooperation in regional health care without mergers or managerial amalgamation.

Despite the accent that will emerge on preventive medicine, there will still be a need for procedures. Thanks to the further development of minimal invasive techniques and pharmaceutical possibilities, the stress on the patient will be reduced further. Day admissions and out-patient treatment will increasingly become the norm. This means that out-patient departments will, in the future, become the heart of the hospital. The hospital will become smaller and will largely cater to patients who require a high- or intensive-care setting. As a result, nursing staff will become specialists. Hospitals will, as a result, become a continuum of specialists.

The future of the European healthcare industry

Deniz Selimen

An old Turkish proverb says, "Call the bear 'Uncle' till you are safe across the bridge." Don't bite the hand that feeds you, one would say in English. For a long time this was reality for patients in Europe, both within and outside the European Union. Doctors and nurses were gods; they were not to be criticized. Right now, European patients are more demanding than ever. This is especially true for the elderly, a group that is growing very fast in Europe. We know that people in their old age cost the healthcare industry much more than young people. A massive growth in the healthcare demand of the elderly is to be expected. This is just one of the trends that will affect the future of European hospitals.

There is more. For instance, health tourism is an up and coming phenomenon. It will be necessary to ship patients to hospitals in low-cost countries in South-East Europe. This will not only happen for operations that are needed for professional medical reasons. Already more and more North-West Europeans are using Turkish hospitals for plastic surgery. More will follow, to Rumania, Bulgaria and other countries in this area. The local hospitals in North-West Europe will only be used for emergencies, and will tend to specialize in certain fields. The trend of part-time living described in this book will enhance this process. European health insurance companies must be alive to the opportunities for health tourism.

Technology will also change the hospital of the future. With new technologies for operations, it is possible for a surgeon in a hospital in Paris to direct an operation on a patient in a hospital in Istanbul through the Internet (a process known as telemedicine). Since smaller operating equipment is used, the scars are smaller and recovery happens quicker. This means lower costs for hospitals.

Since there were major advances in transplant surgery, there has been an unexpected increase in the demand for therapy for end-stage organ-failure patients in Europe. Transplants are a high-cost medical procedure. Increasing health expenditure is forcing governments to cut budgeted expenses as much as possible.

Shipping patients to hospitals in low-cost countries for transplant surgery is a good idea. Performing transplant surgery in low-cost countries may reduce the cost and the increasing demands from those on the unexpectedly crowded waiting lists. But ethical issues and regulations must be taken into consideration. Research into xenotransplantation looks promising. In the near feature organs harvested from genetically modified animals may help patients waiting for transplants. The construction of genetically modified animal farms near to hospitals will perhaps be more than a science fiction fantasy.

Unfortunately terrorism will create many more victims in Europe in the next few years. Hospitals everywhere in Europe should be prepared for this. Attacks by Al Qaeda-inspired terrorists can occur everywhere, as we have experienced in Istanbul, Madrid, Amsterdam and London, and more attacks will follow. Prevention of (severe) casualties will therefore become one of the new key tasks of the hospital of the future. The hospital of the future should also be prepared to treat casualties from terrorist attacks using chemical and biological weapons.

A united European disaster organization should be created. Turkey has survived two major earthquakes, and Greece experienced one major earthquake in 1999. All European countries should combine to produce a multinational disaster relief organization.

In the hospital of the future more work will be taken over by computers and robots, yet the human factor will remain the most important one. Medical–ethical questions will dominate. Who will decide if an 80-year-old can get a new pacemaker or plastic hip? And who will pay for it? Which bear will we call 'Uncle'?

Professor Dr Deniz Selimen RN PhD (1986) is professor of healthcare issues at the Marmara University in Istanbul, Turkey and director of Marmara University College of Nursing.

A spiritual revolution: old and new gods and spirits

According to the most recent statistics, people are becoming more religious. The number of adherents to the major religions is increasing relatively faster than the world population, while numbers of non-religious people and atheists are stagnating. The annual growth in the non-religious (0.8 per cent a year) and atheists (0.2 per cent) is far lower than the growth of the world population (1.2 per cent). Of the major religions, Islam is growing fastest, at a rate of 2.1 per cent. The growth in the number of Christians (1.3 per cent) is only just higher than the growth of the world population. The number of Buddhists decreases annually by 1 per cent (source: www.kuleuven.be).

These are worldwide figures. In Europe things are somewhat different. It is true that the number of religious people is increasing in Europe, but in a different direction. In the introductory chapter we mentioned that many people no longer believe in "God" but in "something". This is particularly true in North-West Europe; in Eastern Europe there is as yet no sign of it. In a large part of Europe, religion has never really gone away. In Italy, Spain and Poland, Catholicism has (despite the secularization) remained part of culture and life. The same is true in Eastern Europe, for example the Orthodox Church in Bulgaria. And in fact the same is true in North-West Europe, where the majority is Protestant Christian, with a few Catholic minorities.

In this part of Europe, the attitude to religion and spirituality has changed during the last few decades. Spirituality in these regions of Europe is in fact encapsulated in citizenship. If you trip over in this part of Europe, strangers will help you back on your feet. Citizenship is spirituality, and you don't need a God for that. God is in the citizens and in the way we deal with each other. That has had consequences for formal religious structures and institutions. Many churches emptied, and many young people were no longer brought up on religion. But as we have said, religion is something that everybody needs.

In the Middle Ages, art served religion. Artists produced murals and stained-glass windows for churches, architects created masterpieces in their religious buildings, and sculptors, painters and other artists produced much religious art. Now art has an

autonomous-religious function. In the 21st century, you can get inspiration from secular art: a painting, a sculpture, a carpet. This allowed autonomous art to flourish. Europeans are spending more and more money on art. More Europeans from all social layers are visiting museums, and people are buying art objects for their homes, offices and country house. People are surrounding themselves with art as they used to surround themselves with religion. Religious values and norms still live in citizenship. And the way in which we regard new technology also has something sacred about it; religious, even.

In these European areas, God is now back, certainly among the young, but not necessarily in the traditional way. Many believe in "something" between heaven and hell. This something can be a god, but it could also be something else spiritual.

In countries such as China, the demise of communism has made way for religion. The way in which Christians react to this can have enormous political implications. Christian missionaries have set their sights on this densely populated area, certainly following their successes in South Korea and South Vietnam, where a large part of the population has converted to Christianity in the last few decades.

It is an illusion to believe that the relatively areligious parts of Europe will stay as they are in a world that is becoming increasingly religious. Radical Islam cannot be combated by atheism but only by another religion. It is also an illusion to believe that we shall only have to deal with the new dominance of Asia in the economic field; the power of Asia will also be felt in religion and spirituality.

New mythos

This is beginning to make itself felt in the least religious countries of the European Union, particularly among the young. Religious symbols (such as a cross on a chain around the neck) are reappearing in public, partly as a reaction to the dominant presence of Islam in the form of headscarves and traditionally designed mosques. The new religion does not stand in isolation. Every person has a need for *logos* (rational matters, such as science, technology, and economy) and *mythos* (inspiration, religion, spirituality). Non-religious people can find *mythos* in art or nature, sex or other spiritual sources. The elite flirt with Buddhism: you will find a statue of Buddha in many households in the higher economic category. This has no direct implications, but it could be that Buddhism will become the religion of the elite, while the lower social classes hold firm to their existing religions. Buddhism is chic, and what's more, once China becomes a superpower, the elite will already have connections with that country.

At the same time, it is traditionally true that in times of great technological and scientific progress there is an automatic resurgence of religion. At the very moment that people start doing things that they thought were ruled or determined by God – flying in an airplane or travelling to the moon – they begin wondering if there is more between heaven and earth. And now that we are becoming more and more successful in tampering with our bodies, our lives, and with all sorts of artificial procedures that can improve our bodies and extend our life expectancy, we start asking ourselves where life came from and what happens when it is over. This is certainly true now that we can postpone the end, and once we become older. When will the moment come when we do not die any more? When, thanks to medical science and gene technology we can replace, renew or give new impulses to parts of our bodies, so that we live longer? If we automate death out of our lives, is there still a god? If women can soon have children without the intervention of the male, what will be the consequences for the balance between the sexes? People try to find answers to questions such as these in religion.

A spiritual battlefield in Europe?

Minne Buwalda

Ten years ago, we would never have suspected that religious tensions in Western Europe would have been a hot item in the media. Religious struggle is considered by many as a rearguard action, as an atavism that will quickly disappear, but it now stands in the spotlight again in the shape of a conflict between Islam and (mainly Christian) modernity. Religion and spirituality have returned to Europe in the 21st century. It is all about both traditional and totally new religions. That the struggle on the spiritual level is far livelier than was thought for a long time is shown by a recent item in a Dutch newspaper. A number of Buddhist monks had made a sand mandala in a church in the Dutch provincial city of Amersfoort. It was part of a cultural exchange programme, but it met with virulent resistance from the Evangelical congregation in the town. They warned that simply looking at the art work could cause "serious damage to mind and body", because the sand sculpture was a "palace for demons". They started a "prayer offensive" in order to "fight back in the heavenly regions". Now as far as I know, Buddhism is one religion that has little interest in missionary activities, certainly when compared with other conversion religions such as Islam or Christianity; these Christians, however, obviously thought differently. And you could also feel sorry for them, because they have to not only fight off the many threats of Islam, but also struggle against the idols and demons of other religions – and in our multicultural society, there are plenty of those around. Every group that chooses to come and live here brings along its own gods and goddesses. The "heavenly region" will become one huge battlefield.

Everybody knows that a mixed marriage can bring forth beautiful children; but it is less well known that a mingling of religious systems can result in a beautiful spiritual marriage. Take the Santo Daime religion from Brazil. The symbols used in this faith are through-and-through Catholic, with considerable adoration of

Jesus and Mary. But it also works with spirit practices from African religions, and the central aspect of the teaching – the drinking of the hallucinogenic *ayahuasca* – originated in the Amazon basin in Brazil itself. Indigenous people there have, for thousands of years, sought healing and contact with the other side through visions induced by this bitter-tasting brew. During church services, highly disciplined song and dance is performed from sunset to sunrise, and this results in a collective mystic experience.

The Daimist congregation which arose in recent years in the rainforests of Brazil is strongly focused on ecological awareness and sustainable economic development. And in the meantime the teaching is becoming global, certainly in Europe, with official churches in Spain, France, the Netherlands, and Italy; earlier a foothold was secured in the United States. Whether the Santo Daime service is held in a tiny hall in the suburbs of Paris or in a church on the polder in the Dutch countryside, you are confronted during the ritual with a spirit world and visions that are not from here, but have their origins in the Brazilian jungle. Was the Evangelical congregation right when they saw in the sand mandala a "palace of demons"?

Minne Buwalda (the Netherlands) studied philosophy. He is a publicist and editor at Van Gennep Publishers in Amsterdam

Religious experience

In the 21st century, the new religious experience in Europe will probably show the following pattern. Buddhism will win ground, certainly among the older people who belong to the higher social classes. Belief in spirits, ghosts, in short the supernatural, will increase. In Britain and South America and Indonesia it is a traditional part of the culture; those in the more sober parts of Europe have never really wanted to get involved. Belief in an after-life decreased when, in the 1960s, people became increasingly divorced from the church. Angels, demons, spirits: these no longer had a place in our rational world. They do have a place in the Asiatic world, the new epicentre of world power. Europeans will have to slowly but surely adapt to this.

But a greater belief in spirits goes deeper. It is also an answer to the continuing desire (even among non-believers) for spirituality and a certain contact, communication, with "the other side". That explains the increase in mediums, fortune tellers and spiritual leaders. Islamic immigrants traditionally consult fortune tellers, and an increasing number of indigenous Europeans are also doing this. And they will continue doing this, no matter how much these women (and the occasional man) are castigated by the established church. Fortune telling is becoming modernized: you can have your horoscope drawn by computer. Talking to trees, mice and the like is not in favour with the young, who find it all too airy-fairy, but Eastern methods, such as acupuncture, shiatsu, acupressure and the like have a growing following. The use of new mind-changing substances is also increasing, and will become a permanent part of our lifestyle now and in the future.

Traditionally, Europe has an alcohol culture; immigration brought us people from drug cultures. In Europe, you drink a beer or a glass of wine with friends and you do business over meals where the wine flows. Alcohol is the lubricant of bonding. In other cultures, drugs are the lubricant. In Yemen, you chew on qat with your friends and business acquaintances, in Arabic countries you share a water-pipe, and in old China you used opium. The Indians of South America used drugs obtained from a variety of plants to contact the spirit world. Brazilian religions, such as Candomblé and Umbanda – a mixture of Catholicism and rituals from Indian and African religions – which are now growing in Europe also make use of drugs. At the start of the church service, people drink a cup of a bitter, hallucinatory herbal mixture and then the rhythmic mass gets under way.

We live in an age in which alcohol and drug cultures are intermingling, and in which the use of new artificial drugs such as Ecstasy is growing. A comparison with the old Indian cultures in which drugs were used to induce a trance and thus come into contact with the world of spirits and gods is not out of place. Perhaps in the new, more spiritual Europe, we shall need a new mind-enhancing drug-mix that suits the current age, its population and these trends. Perhaps it will be a new artificial drug with an alcohol flavour?

The number of atheists, nihilists and agnostics is decreasing. Since an international religious conflict (Islam versus the West) is approaching, impartiality is no longer acceptable. This group of non-believers can, without losing face, embrace Buddhism or the new multi-religions, such as the Brazilian Candomblé and Umbanda. Christianity is making a comeback among the young, although in different forms and variants. Catholicism is having a revival, certainly supported by the election of a new pope. In the future the pope will almost certainly be chosen from one of the BRIC (Brazil, Russia, India, China) countries.

Catholicism

Catholicism is growing in Asia, where it is considered by many to be a salvation religion. In South Korea and South Vietnam it has already become the most important religion, and has taken the place of Buddhism. In India too, the church is growing slowly but surely. On Bali, Catholicism is winning from Hinduism. One of the reasons is that it offers ex-Hindus salvation from the caste system.

Catholicism has many features and characteristics which, if properly used, can promote the enormous economic growth of the religion in the 21st century. To begin with, it has a large show and camp element about it. With its glitter and glamour, dresses, statues, stained-glass windows, and incense, (high) mass becomes a marvellous show. In a time when entertainment is so important to society, this is a definite advantage. In addition, the Catholic Church has a clear structure of authority, something that other churches lack. It is logical, since it is a copy of the old organizational structure of the Roman Empire: the emperor becomes the pope, the senate becomes the curia, and so on. In chaotic times, this offers clarity and tranquillity, certainly if the Islamic caliphate is reinstated and with it an Islamic "pope". That will require a powerful counterbalance in the West, and who better equipped for this than the Catholic pope?

In that case, a solution must be found for the problems of clerical celibacy and the sexual excesses this causes. It is rather awkward if you have to put half your clerics in prison because of sexual misuse of children. And all that compensation costs the church enormous amounts of money. An euro can only be spent once, so it is better to make a deep investment in the church rather than spend it on compensation. Now the church is being castigated, and that is not good for its image or its further growth. The best solution is to abolish celibacy and also get rid of homophobia. Gay people are frequently wonderful showmen and can greatly enhance the camp content of the church. What's more, the church is riddled with gays, even if that is not openly admitted. Another advantage is that the Catholic Church has a number of clearly identifiable symbols, such as a cross and chain, that fit in with a whole range of fashion styles. At the start of the 21st century, the cross is hipper than ever and is increasingly found in jewellery, T-shirts, and various designs for today's youth.

Protestantism

At the same time, the religious experience among Protestants is also growing. The trend will continue, and generations are growing up that are much more religious that the previous two generations, particularly that of the baby-boomers. This is not leading to more people going to church: the new religious experience is totally separate from this. Cyber-pastors take the place of the live preachers of times past, and the need for mass meetings of like-minded people is not satisfied by the weekly harness of Sunday church services. On the other hand, people are once again having their children christened. In the mass media there is now a market for television preachers, who reassuringly address the people and spiritually guide them through these uncertain times, which are characterized by all the changes that are taking place and have to be given a place in our lives.

In the Netherlands, people used to have G. B. J. Hilterman, an old radio commentator with considerable stature who reassured the nation every Sunday, discussed the changes taking place in the world, and thus kept things in their proper perspective. In America, the "anchors" of television stations acted in much the same way, and of course so did the television ministers. In 21st-century Europe, there is a market for new multimedia evangelicals, who do not necessarily belong to a religious denomination or parish. They could even be atheists, but they have to be rooted in the technological revolution, have charisma, embody progressive thinking, and have a reassuring, meditative, and at the same time enthusiastic effect on people. In one area of Europe they will be politicians or political rock stars, in other areas they will be classical preachers from a classic church, and in yet others they will be anchors for mass media (an integration of television, the Internet and live performances).

An example of such a new preacher is Tariq Ramadan, a preacher for European Muslims who lives in Switzerland, and who acts for many European Muslims as a sort of Islamic pope. European security services, by the way, do not trust him; he is considered the humane face of Al Qaeda. In the Netherlands, the murdered politician Pim Fortuyn acted as the new preacher, in Argentine it was Eva Peron, in England Princess Diana and subsequently David Beckham. In the United States Oprah Winfrey has now achieved this status, in Germany Christiane Sabinsen, in France Nicolas Sarkozy. In South Africa there are Desmond Tutu and Nelson Mandela, and the Dalai Lama has this stature, even for non-Tibetans.

In the future, we shall have more of such spiritual leaders who represent modernity (and morality) and fill in our need for *mythos*. Do not forget: the most important themes in the coming time will have to do with morality. Who in the future will decide how long people with severe dementia are kept alive? And whether a demented grandmother of 80 deserves a new artificial hip? And who pays? The technological revolution brings back morality into our everyday lives, and religious and spiritual movements will remain the keepers of morality, even in 21st century Europe. Classical contradictions will also be broken down. Orthodox Jews, Muslims and Christians joined together in 2005 to prevent a large-scale parade of gay people through Jerusalem. In the Netherlands there was something similar at the end of the 20th century when a number of groups demonstrated to oppose the euthanasia legislation proposed by the government.

Converts and new religions

The number of converts will grow, in various directions: Muslims who become Catholics, Protestants who become Catholics, but also

Catholics who become Muslims and Christians who become Buddhists. Humanism only has a future if it no longer labels itself – as it does now – as an alternative to religion. It has to coexist with religion, and only then will it have a future market.

Eras such as the current one, with rapid scientific and technological change, are frequently eras that see the emergence of new religions. The religion of the Sikhs in India arose in such a period, and so too did Buddhism. It is quite possible that a new religion will now appear that will attract a large number of followers. That could be a sect (as yet obscure) in California that suddenly breaks through in the West (as previously happened on a limited scale with Bhagwan). It could be a new politician or pop star who suddenly achieves a prophetic or almost divine status, such as happened in the Netherlands with Pim Fortuyn.

Environmental revolution and Latinizing the culture

The climate will change, but moderately. The environmental revolution will not hit all European countries: only Belgium and the Netherlands are below sea level, and they will have to contend with wet feet. Venice too will have to face this: St Mark's Square will regularly be under water. The European rivers will rise a little.

None of this will be as dramatic as was predicted by the Club of Rome in 1972. The UN's *Millennium Assessment* published in 2005 is relatively level-headed about it all. In certain areas, we are making too heavy demands on the environment, but is this serious? The United States and Europe cut down their original forests and polluted the air as they struggled to get their economies going. Once Europe had earned enough money, its governments set about cleaning the air, the land and water. The writers of the *Millennium Assessment* are correct in saying that environmental problems are a side-effect of poverty. But economic growth is ultimately the solution, as we are now seeing in Asia: richer countries are better able to tackle environmental problems. In poor countries, survival is all that matters. What do you think they prefer to do in Asia, eat or admire butterflies? A Chinese writer recently summarized it very succinctly:

> When it suited you in Europe to overtax the environment in order to fuel your economic progress, that was fine. But now we are doing the same, it is suddenly bad for the environment. Is your environmental mafia not involved in maintaining the world's economic status quo by using pious texts?

Despite our love of pointing the accusatory finger at developing countries, we are not fully committed to the environment. Environmental issues are included in European treaties, but national interests appear to be more important. All member states want their economies to grow, so the environment remains an undernourished child.

What's more, there is also the question of whether global warming is due to the emission of carbon dioxide. Many are convinced that changes in climate are perfectly normal; in the Middle Ages, Europe was on average warmer than it is today, and in the 20th century there were differences in temperature that could not be explained by extra emissions of carbon dioxide. A good book about this problem is *State of Fear* by Michael Crichton, in which scientists and environmentalists fight each other for the truth about the rising sea level.

Outdoors culture

In North-West Europe it is becoming warmer, with milder winters and longer summers. This means that we spend more of our time in the open air. We are developing a pavement café culture; our social life takes place outside: this represents the Latinizing of our culture. Traditionally, North-West Europe had an indoors culture, because of its cool climate. Many houses in North-West Europe do not have access to an outside area; it was not necessary, said the architects of the past. It was always cold! We looked on in amazement at immigrants from warm countries such as Morocco and Turkey, countries with a well-developed outdoors life. Should children be allowed to stay up so late? Why were they allowed to stay outside so much? Now we all want it.

Security

It is difficult to marry our desire to spend more of our lives outside with our feelings of insecurity and the urge to cocoon; we thus desire a safe outdoors, free of petty criminals, pickpockets and other types of lowlife. If this cannot be offered in public places, then we have to move to public places within gated communities. Housing cooperatives would be sensible to have a rooftop garden installed in their complex, with a beach and a swimming pool, neatly fenced off and protected, and only accessible to owners and their guests. Then users will not need to sit in traffic tailbacks to get to and from the beach, or to sunbathe in public parks in fear of being mugged, and can still enjoy the open air. Balconies, terraces and flat roofs will increasingly become an integral part of our living space, of our house. But the Latinizing of the North-West European culture goes further: we have a greater desire to go out, to have fun, to be entertained and to relax in the open air. There will be a bigger market for open-air terraces, and events in the open air, such as the Love Parade in Berlin, where people can dance, watch, be admired, drink, flirt, party, and behave like animals. That will also be noticeable in the music: more Latin influences will be felt in Northern European music, and Latino icons (like J-Lo and Ricky Martin) will capture our hearts.

Going out = dressing up

In this, the Northern European and Southern European lifestyles are moving closer to each other. The Southern European "promenading" behaviour is now also seen in Northern Europe. But there isn't much point in promenading if you don't look your best; the cosmetics industry will do big business. In the past few years, Europe has been in the throes of an economic recession, but people did not economize on make-up or plastic surgery; these flourished as never before. The market for food has stagnated, but the cosmetic giant Procter & Gamble has grown. In a Latinized culture with much of its life spent in the open air, the emphasis is

on looking good, with as few wrinkles, spots and blemishes as possible. People want perfect skins, attractive lips and mouths, accentuated eyes and make-up (for both men and women) that draw attention to the positive features of their face and body and camouflage the less attractive features. Investors can make a healthy profit from shares in the cosmetic industry.

Closely allied to this is the market for plastic surgery. That too is flourishing in this era when almost everything can be made and rebuilt – including our own bodies. We are swallowing more slimming pills. The market for new luxury clothing is growing. That is luxury casual clothing that can also be worn at formal functions; it is suitable for trendy seniors and hip youngsters with a well-filled bank account. At the same time, the market for good cheap clothing, often made in low-wage countries, is also growing. And making your own clothes, or having them made by local tailors according to your own designs, or as copies of the clothes featured in fashion magazines, is also on the increase.

Foreigners and gays are the trendsetters, others follow. In the course of their lives young men today have become metro-sexual – fashion-conscious heterosexuals. Boys born now are conditioned from the cradle to become metro-sexual. In warm countries, such as Italy, Spain, France and Portugal, people always took pride in their appearance. In fact, Italy has changed the rest of Europe more than America has: Italians taught us to love design, taught us that going through life well dressed is wonderful, and gave us pizzas and pasta, designer kitchens and designer furniture – taught us, in fact, that form made the content something special. One of the reasons why women in these warm Catholic countries (nearer to the Vatican) have gone on birth strike (women there have fewer children than women in the rest of Europe) is that the ladies prefer to spend their money on dressing up, going out and designer goods, rather than on screaming bambinos, who ruin their figures and cost handfuls of money – money they would rather spend on other things. Here again: you can only spend each euro once, and people have to set their priorities in this experience economy. Going through life bambino-free allows room for design. They have really understood this in Italy.

Nature

The warming of the earth leads to a rise in the sea and the rivers. That demands a different type of water management. It seems not unlikely that certain coastal areas in the Netherlands, Belgium, Italy and Greece will in the future have to be evacuated because of the rising water, so measures are essential, for example in the form of dykes to hold back the sea. A Pentagon study is rather sombre about this: within a few decades, it suggests, new dykes will be essential in these areas of Europe. Other environmental studies suggest that it will be at least 150 years before it is necessary. It all depends on what you believe.

In North-West Europe, the milder winters and longer summers are already having an effect on flora and fauna. Species that previously did not appear in these areas are now moving up from the south. Dolphins are now seen more frequently in the North Sea. In Amsterdam, there are large colonies of rose-ringed parakeets.

During 2004 in the Netherlands, more than 50 species of plants were added to the standard list, plus 48 new species of slugs. According to the book *Opgewarmd Nederland* (Warmed up Holland) by Jan van Arkel (2004), the climate border shifts 11 metres each day. Because of this, species that prefer cold climates are moving farther north (to Denmark, Sweden, Norway and the north of Great Britain) and the Netherlands and Belgium now welcome several species from the south. Should we be concerned about this? Yes and no. Yes, because we will also entertain less welcome visitors such as blue algae, and new diseases. No, because climate change has always been with us: in the Middle Ages North-West Europe was a lot warmer, and the sea frequently washed over the coastal areas of the Low Countries.

In Southern Europe, there will be shortages of fresh water and

more areas will turn into desert. A lot of course can be done about this. Fresh-water streams can be moved along newly dug canals, fresh water can be distilled from sea water (as already takes place in Israel and Dubai), and it is also possible to recycle water. Modern cruise ships already do this: used water from toilets, washbasins and bathrooms is purified and reused. These techniques will soon be used on shore. There will soon be a large market for recycling water in the home, if the price for fresh water rises far enough. What's more, "fresh-water pockets" in the sea have been discovered in various places throughout the world, such as along the coast of Saudi Arabia. At sea, often hundreds of metres below the surface level, there are reserves of fresh water in the salt water, known as fresh-water pockets. They are, of course, not actual pockets, but water reserves that remain separate from the salt water. At the moment it is too expensive to exploit these, but if fresh water becomes expensive enough, the exploitation will become profitable. The Saudis are already looking into this, much to the dismay of Uruguay, which has one of the largest fresh-water reserves in the world and thought that this "new gold" would bring golden times in the 21st century. But still, shipping fresh water from Uruguay to Southern Europe remains an option. Uruguay was founded by the Spaniards, so why shouldn't they drench the old homeland in the 21st century? Everybody in Spain could drink from the Uruguay water trough!

Temporary building

Because of climate change, different building and living possibilities will arise. But temporary buildings will also appear, because history teaches us that climate change such as we are now undergoing is always followed by a period of cooling down. Decades of increasing temperatures are followed by decades of colder temperatures. Some suggest that the Gulf Stream that determines our climate will cease in the future, which will result in the average temperature in parts of Europe dropping considerably. Temporary building, rather than building for posterity, is more sensible. For the moment this means wooden prefabricated buildings, conventional wooden buildings, and buildings of impregnated cardboard. The "sustainable building" which is now in fashion is actually out of date, no longer suitable to the current age, and not as sustainable as the name suggests.

Building for the future will have a new dimension in the 21st century. I recently saw the concrete of the future in a cement factory. Concrete floors and walls have hollow pipes in them, and on the roofs of the buildings constructed from this new type of concrete there are water pumping installations. Water is pumped out of the ground, through the pipes in the house, and provides natural air-conditioning, which is very practical and should be suitable for housing in the near future. In India and Iran buildings used to make use of water as a means of cooling, and it is interesting that this concept is now returning in a new guise. Houses will also be built in a different direction, no longer tending north–south with glass patio doors on the south, because rooms on the south cannot be kept cool; living rooms would turn into saunas, and combining a sauna with a living-room is taking things a little too far in the experience economy.

Conclusion

This is a nicely integrated megatrend: technology changes our lifestyle, our lives will be lived in a different climate, and there is a new spirituality that allows us to manage this and give it all a place in our lives in 21st-century Europe. In fact, every one of us plays the starring role in his or her own film. You can share this with all sorts of people, through your own website, by participating in real-life soaps, by being prepared to sacrifice privacy in a whole range of areas. Life will be one long Muppet show.

Megatrend **4**
The citizen in the lead

All European countries have some kind of welfare system. This meant that until the 1990s many European governments, in particular those in Northern Europe, increasingly transferred activities from the private sector to the public sector. The welfare state enjoyed a golden era. Child care, something that was traditionally sorted out by parents, became a task of the government. The same was true of care of the elderly: grandmother was put into a state-run elderly people's or nursing home and no longer cared for by her family. State involvement is now becoming a thing of the past. Governments are withdrawing from these areas – largely for financial reasons – and the welfare state is being reduced. In the framework of the economic progression envisaged for Europe that was laid down in the Lisbon agenda of 2000, member states were expected to reduce their expenditure on welfare.

Families will thus play a larger role. This can do no harm. One of the reasons that there is no welfare state in Asia, not even in communist China, is because there is a fear that this could lead to the disintegration of the family. That is exactly what has happened in Europe in the last few decades. Family members generally treat each other in the same way as people would treat their friends – nothing more, nothing less. They maintain their contacts with each other for a variety of emotional and economic reasons. Once these no longer exist, there is no real impetus to maintain family relationships, and often that was the case. Now that the government is taking a less prominent place, families will become more important again. The citizen is now taking over tasks from the government.

In politics, too, citizens are having more say in things, largely because they have become more aware. Thanks partly to the Internet, citizens are able to investigate things for themselves and form their own opinions. Thanks to communities on the Net there is a degree of collective opinion forming that directs itself against established politics. New politicians with one-liners and charisma conquer the political arena, with the support of the public, and the old politics has to leave the field.

In short: a trend can be discerned away from governmental involvement towards collective opinion-forming and the end of the welfare state. In the meantime there is also a noticeable individualization taking place. Young people in particular clearly show that they want to go their own way, no longer allowing themselves to be influenced by the spirit of the times, but instead making their own choices. Young people think it more important to be an individual than to belong to a group. They prefer to maintain family relationships. Young people are a good measure of how individualization is proceeding. We take a closer look at their world at the end of this chapter.

The end of the welfare state: back to family life

In the 21st century, the citizen is in the lead: citizens are taking control of the organization and management of their lives. Because of this, family life will take on a new guise. An important change is the introduction of the "rush-hour family", also known as the "sandwich family", in which partners take care of each other, their

children and their elderly parents. This also includes taking care of childless aunts or elderly uncles whose children have emigrated abroad.

The rush-hour family will become the cornerstone of society. Their lifestyle and the way they organize their days will be different from those of "normal" families. What will change? During the week, life will be organized as efficiently as possible. Much use will be made of technology, and all sorts of convenience products will be used, so that the many activities – the rush hour – can be managed. That means, for example, that during the week there will seldom be time to cook elaborate meals. Ready-prepared meals from the supermarket, easily prepared food, or take-aways (which are rapidly proliferating in large cities) will be used a lot.

Take-aways will change. There will be kilo restaurants, a sort of take-away where the food is prepared in large dishes. Customers fill a plastic dish and pay per kilo. Whether they take a kilo of potatoes or a kilo of pasta or rice mixed with sauce, it doesn't make much difference. The kilo price is the same. Such shops already exist in Brazil and New York, but now, thanks to ethnic entrepreneurship in large cities, they are also making their appearance in Europe. They are a godsend for rush-hour families: fast, cheap and healthy. The wok restaurant also satisfies this need.

Another possibility is that food pills will replace meals during the week. Already a lot of people use food supplements; in the near future people will be able to use meal substitutes during the week. Since the world population will grow during the coming 45 years, and regular agriculture, livestock farming and the like will not be able – at least without biotechnological assistance – to satisfy the growing demand, a chemically produced food pill will be a good alternative.

In contrast, the weekend will become an oasis of peace and hospitality. Then elaborate meals will be on the menu, for the rush-hour family and its friends. Slow cooking will be the norm. People will cocoon, garden, spend time in the open air, but also take part in the nightlife of the cities: weekends will become a mini-holiday. In this way, the holiday feeling becomes an integrated part of our daily lives. The strict division between work and holiday will become more vague. Because an increasing number of people from the higher social classes have two houses, which allow them to experience two lifestyles simultaneously in the new experience economy, they will be able to spend their cocoon weekends either in their place in the country, or in their house in the busy city. This will mean that people take holidays less frequently: the energy and impulses that people get from the holiday feeling will be integrated into their daily life.

School and care

The school system will change. Children and young people will attend school or study part-time, as we mentioned earlier; in the remaining time, they will carry out care responsibilities as a sort of community service. That implies a longer period at school. Primary school will stay as it is now, but once children go to secondary school and on to higher education, they will have to undertake care tasks in addition to their school work. They will therefore enter the employment market at a later age than now.

At the same time, citizens will invest more in their health and in prevention of illness, partly with the use of medical bio and gene technologies and by the introduction of preventive medicines. Since it is no longer the government that makes these investments but the citizens themselves, this will give rise to a class system. Part of the population will be excluded since they will not be able to afford all these novelties. Professor Dr Wim de Ridder calls this the genetic struggle between the haves and the have-nots, the DNA divide. According to him, the fight is far from over.

Care tourism

Recuperation from operations and other procedures will take place more frequently at home and in care hotels rather than in expensive hospitals. But care tourism will also come into being: elderly people needing care from North Europe will allow themselves to be spoiled in Southern Europe, where people speak their language and the costs are cheaper than in clinics back home. What's more, in the nursing homes in Southern Europe there is accommodation for the patient's family, who can spend the night. In North-West Europe families are not (yet) welcome in nursing homes.

Care tourism will increase significantly in the coming decades. Having operations performed abroad – for example, having plastic surgery while enjoying a holiday in Thailand – will also be more prevalent in the future than it is now. This will drastically change the face of health care. Home carers will have technological aids with which they can report electronically the condition of the patient to headquarters. Freelance home carers will take over part of the work from existing home care institutions, individually or as members of a collective practice. Personal budgets (PBs) will become more common, and relieve the pressure on home care; voluntary aid, whether free or paid, will once again make an appearance. Voluntary work in the care sector will increase.

The LHD plan

Even death will become a personal responsibility. Something like dementia will raise important medical ethical questions, which will cause heated public discussion: is euthanasia justified in certain cases? Citizens will probably come up with their own solutions for this in practice, such as a personal euthanasia arrangement. Before they start to suffer from dementia, they will hand over the management of their estate and other business concerns to an agency, which will then manage everything for a modest fee, saving them from having to burden their family and friends. Every citizen will have his or her own plan for life, health and death: the LHD plan. They will reach agreement about this with their health insurer and their nearest and dearest, and everybody should be happy.

New citizenship

Family will play an increasingly important role, and government will move further into the background (arguably it will be forced to do this). This will give society a totally different look. A new sort of collectivism will arise, partly fuelled by successive technological developments, says de Ridder. Thanks to interactive media, we should collectively stay abreast of what is happening in the world and form our own opinions about this. For society, this means that power is now shared among many different organizations. This is not a pleasant prospect for the social elite. As self-organization

becomes more important, the power of the elite will diminish. This new society is characterized by Harlan Cleveland, the American political scientist and public executive, as the "nobody-in-charge" society; the Internet and the international monetary market are examples of this.

With the introduction of each new generation of information technology (and that will happen every two to three years), our society will become less centrally managed. The reason for this is that the products that people buy and exchange will become increasingly more "virtual". When a physical product is purchased, there is a change of ownership. If an idea, a vision, an opinion is sold, both the old and new owner possess it. Cleveland says: "If it's a thing, it's exchanged; if it's information, it's shared." The transformation that we are currently experiencing is due to the fact that the most important source of assistance, the Internet, is shared by billions of people.

The ideal image of an independent person with a protected private life and unique thoughts, knowledge and opinions is thus no longer realistic. George Orwell saw that as a threat to the individual. Susan Greenfield, an English professor with particular interest in the workings of the mind, says that the human mind is the personification of a person's experiences. She maintains that the more experience a person gains and gives personal meaning to, the higher the status achieved and the more important somebody becomes. She adds that information technology has an unprecedented influence on our experiences, and enables people to shape their minds in the way they see fit. This leads to a collective ego. Terror caused by the Nazis or by Al Qaeda is the terror not of people who do not know what they are doing, but of people with a strong group mentality and a clear set of values. The cause of the Second World War is often attributed to the fact that, after the First World War, the German people were unable to exist as private individuals. This was cleverly exploited. The communists, too, believe in the supreme power of the collective. In the 20th century, the private ego defeated the collective ego; in the 21st century the reverse will be true.

In his essay "Globalization: blessing or curse?" Wim Smit, a Dutch publicist, couples this phenomenon with globalization. This is something that initially was only associated with multinationals, such as Coca-Cola and McDonald's, but now also refers to the way we define citizenship. Ultimately, the latter is a consequence of the former. Smit comments:

> People witnessed a government that was constantly retreating, that handed over many tasks and responsibilities to private enterprise, and thus ultimately became employed by private business. The citizens, on the other hand, had elected that government in a democratic manner and now saw their position as citizen transformed into one of consumer and became,

through a non-democratic position in corporate life, the producer of the products and services of private enterprise. In addition, the necessary steps were taken to transfer health care and pensions to the private sector, which resulted in a further depreciation of the role of government, and the citizens were given greater responsibility for their health and pension provisions. Thus citizens became, in the long run, investors in themselves, and the awareness is and was created that citizens are producers and consumers and investors. Citizenship has thus changed, and we need hardly be surprised that there are hardly any organizations that are able to represent this new citizenship in an effective way.

Citizens are, according to Smit, eagerly searching for a way in which they can give effective opposition to the private sector and government, since they no longer have any faith in these thanks to pay-rise restrictions and the "grab everything you can" culture. There is also a growing lack of interest in politics. Who should we vote for? Who can be trusted and who will stand up for the rights of the citizen? Smit believes that citizens will have to join forces to combat the effects of globalization.

If we connect this opinion to the ones by de Ridder mentioned earlier, we can conclude that technology will play an important role in this. Smit quotes the Italian philosopher Gianni Vattimo, who says: "The new popular culture of the mass media has not led to increased transparency, either in the political or economic sense; it has led largely to greater chaos and disorder .... It is precisely chaos that offers the best chances for renewal and change." That citizens collectively can achieve a lot is something that few would dispute. And that this process has been taking place for some time in Europe is demonstrated by the impotency of politics, as we shall discuss later: citizens have lost their faith in old politicians and these latter are being replaced by "political pop stars". The citizen in Europe is gradually taking the lead.

Soft power

Thanks to these developments, we see the appearance of the term "soft power". Soft power is the power that is exercised by gaining respect for the aims and the means that are used so that voluntary participation replaces force. The term is attributed to the American political analyst Joseph Nye, who defines it as "the ability of a country to persuade other nations to participate in its aims without applying any force". Soft power is not limited to nation-states. Many non-governmental organizations (NGOs) are based on this power. It is stimulated by the fast

growth of the Internet, resulting in the emergence of political platforms. People thus use the Internet for social aims, and the Net becomes a political platform. The networks that arise have a common cultural identity, religious, political or corporate ethics, or social value. Many are small and will remain so; others grow to large organizations with much economic and political power. These networks will become more important than geographical networks.

The power of the bloggers is interesting in this connection. Increasingly the Internet is becoming a part of the regular world, and provides access to information. Opinion formers will be influenced more often than before by bloggers, people who provide commentary on their weblog about national and global events. Because they have no media behind them and often do not even come out of journalism, they can operate freely and independently. The opinion of the bloggers counts and is accessible for everybody, and thus they become a flea on the hide of the existing authoritative media.

The phenomenon of soft power will be strengthened by the way work is organized. The traditional office, now 150 years old, has had its best time. It is expected that very soon a third of the work force will work from home. An increasing number of people work as freelancers – as independent entrepreneurs – and will not be dependent for their identity and career on those that a company places in charge of them. The number of managers will decrease by 90 per cent in the coming ten years. This development is partly caused by the fact that many employees are extensions of computer-managed production. Robots and other machines change the nature of work. Already 35 per cent of telephone contacts with call centres are handled automatically. Many jobs will disappear.

New work will emerge. Machines have to be installed and programmed, until this "second order" of jobs is also automated. This will result in a "black box" economy, in which a considerable amount of work is automated, and in which people will have to adapt if they wish to continue working. The most stable sector is the care industry. After the industrial and information economies, we are now entering the "care" economy. People are prepared to pay for inter-personal care. Medical care, education and personal service will be the most important job generators.

Back to the shareholder democracy

The old left–right divide in politics will be replaced by a conflict between "old" and "new" politics. Those in power who remain distant and infused with corporate thinking will be replaced by icons of the citizens themselves. And this will result in the corporate democracy becoming a shareholder democracy.

Politics as a recording industry

Many European voters no longer recognize themselves in traditional party politics. Citizens recognize problems and expect politicians to provide a solution, since they believe that they are not capable of doing this themselves. Until now they have frequently been disappointed. The German government has for years been unable to solve the unemployment situation. After each election promises are made, but employment scarcely increases. In Germany right-wing extremists are noticeably more successful than in other European countries.

Because citizens appear to believe that traditional parties are incapable of addressing important issues, there is in many European countries a healthy market for "one-issue parties". These are new political parties that focus on a single issue, have a charismatic leader in charge, and profile themselves extensively in the media. Think of the murdered Pim Fortuyn in the Netherlands, Silvio Berlusconi in Italy, and Jorg Haider in Austria. Feelings of alienation result in an increasing demand for new heroes, new gods, idols, and these are created ever more frequently and creatively, but with an increasingly short shelf-life. They are people who have become folk heroes in ways different from those of traditional politicians, and now take the plunge into politics. For example Pim Fortuyn, who at the start of the 21st century became something of a political pop star in the Netherlands, used to be a prophet, and later turned to politics.

The one-issue politicians of the future will position themselves with a strong personal profile. People who are already well known on television will enter politics, and the personality cult around tomorrow's politicians will be more important than it is at the moment. If this trend continues, European countries will see more and more coalitions between one or more "old" parties and one or more "new" parties. The new political pop stars combine "left" and "right" issues, and this is extremely successful. A left–right discussion within traditional parties has become completely meaningless: voters can be better attracted by a combination of right and left issues and by using political pop stars whom, in the elections, can appeal to both "left" and "right".

This is already evident in various European countries. The cabinet of Anders Fogh Rasmussen came to power in Denmark in 2001, thanks purely to his anti-immigration plans. His centre-right coalition was so successful that, in the general elections of 2005, the coalition parties gained 95 of the 179 parliamentary seats. The government is stable, forward-thinking and progressive, and the population politics it applies are light years ahead of those of other countries. The regulations that restrict immigration work well and are an example for the whole of Europe. In Italy, Silvio Berlusconi did much the same. It is a trend that can also be seen in Turkey (Prime Minister Erdogan came from nowhere to win two-thirds of the parliamentary seats), in Venezuela (where the previously unknown capricious President Chavez gained power democratically), and in the United States (where actor Arnold Schwarzenegger became Governor of California, the sixth largest economy in the world).

"The personal in politics" will be the motto of the politics of the future. The private lives of politicians used to be unimportant. Journalists knew that John Kennedy played around but did not write about it; they thought that improper. The private lives of politicians will become more important than ever as part of their appeal to voters. Politicians who go off the tracks and admit their failings will become popular, just like the former US president Bill

Clinton, who was threatened with impeachment but held on to his position thanks to his popularity with the people.

Social debate

Social debate about important matters takes on new forms under the new political pop stars. The gulf between politics and the citizen is narrowed. New networks of people and organizations that wish to reach agreement about the opinion they have in mind arise in various places and in different forms. An example of such a new form is "The 21st Century Town Meeting", developed by AmericaSpeaks, an institution that organizes various debates in the United States. This model became well known during the discussions about the redevelopment of Lower Manhattan after the attack on the World Trade Center of 11 September 2001. The climax of the debate was held in a conference centre in New York, and 4500 people participated. During the meeting, the Manhattan Development Corporation and the Port Authority presented six plans for the redevelopment of the area. The meeting ended with a declaration rejecting all six proposals. At the same time, the developer was given accurate indications concerning the demands that the new buildings must meet. This made it possible for the first stone to be laid in July 2004, and thus the rebuilding of the Twin Towers got under way.

Another example took place in Germany. In recent times, attempts have been made to involve the public at large in the debate about biotechnology. The initiative was led by the lotto organization Action Mensch. An extensive website, billboards in the major cities, and presentations by well-known personalities from, among other things, German television, highlighted and provided information about various aspects of biotechnology. But there was a lack of debate about the content and there was no commitment from the government or big business.

An attractive option is to combine public actions as described here with the suggestion made by Jean François Rischard of the World Bank, to create global issues networks (GINs). A network made up of governments, companies, private organizations and action groups, should be formed for every major world problem. These groups lay down standards and norms, for example for a responsible attitude towards the environment. Those that do not comply with these standards are publicly humiliated in the media. Reaching agreements and ratifying international treaties often take many years, if not decades, but such networks can operate much more quickly, suggests Rischard. What's more, citizens can identify much more easily with such a network that is concerned with a concrete problem than with a world government or some other abstract bureaucratic institution. It is an idealistic and somewhat haphazard plan, Rischard admits, but the time is ripe for it. "Deep down, people feel that the way in which the world is developing has enormously positive sides, but also terribly negative ones."

Knowledge about how to organize such debates is growing. Larry Susskind, professor at the Massachusetts Institute of Technology (MIT) and frequent author, emphasizes that such participatory processes do not necessarily need to result in any unanimity about the outcome. As an authority in the field of "consensus building", he emphasizes that consensus should be seen as agreement over a proposal that may not offer the best option for everybody, but can be supported by as many people as possible. This allows people from different backgrounds and with different motives to participate in the debate. Collective opinion forming has a future. Wim Smit also couples this with globalization. "Thanks to globalization, almost everything is open to borderless debate."

New youth

If we wish to predict opinion forming, then it is worthwhile taking a closer look at Europe's youth. The future belongs to the young, so

who is more representative than young people? However, sounding their opinions appears easier than it actually is. Young people in the age group 10–18 do not only – logically enough – differ from their parents, but also differ considerably from each other. Prevalent subcultures, such as punks in the 1980s, no longer exist. That people enjoy listening to the same music does not mean they automatically wear the same clothes and view life in the same way. This makes young people seem even more inscrutable than before. These are a number of formative trends concerning the young people of

Western Europe (with thanks to Wim de Ridder). (We discuss the young people of Eastern Europe in Megatrend 7.)

Trend 1 *Belief in the free-market economy*

In the 1990s, belief in the free-market economy had its heyday in Europe. Governments withdrew their participation, and people were convinced that the free-market economy was the solution for everything. "The polluter pays," "the user pays," and "the market takes care of efficiency" were much-heard statements at the time. The world seemed to be developing according to economic principles. From a Western perspective, the 1990s were peaceful years. The world seemed manageable, and the Western, free-economy way of thinking superior. "Making" the world was a matter of liberalization, trade and freedom of expression. Major threats seemed to be permanently eradicated; it was an era without fear.

Young people who grew up in this period expected much of the "here and now" and were never apprehensive about the future. The belief in "makeability" was translated into the high demands they make on products and services offered by companies. Young people want to feel that they are worth something and that companies are willing to satisfy their demands. Loyalty to a brand is only sensible if it has direct tangible consequences. Otherwise, they won't bother. The European youth that grew up in this period experienced an unprecedented growth in prosperity. Getting rich was simply a case of "economic thinking". Other, less profitable activities do not lead to riches, but that was a matter of personal choice. The future was not determined by fate, but was simply a matter of choice. There was no fear of the future. Lack of fear in combination with a "faith in makeability" characterized the 1990s. These were totally different from the sombre and anxious 1980s. This has resulted in considerable differences between today's 20 and 30-year-olds.

Trend 2 *Belief in the pragmatic individual*

The 1990s were pragmatic. There was no room in the economic pragmatism for collective opinions; the individual was central. In education, emphasis also shifted to the individual. Personality and the freedom of the child were of primary importance. The "negotiated family", in which the children could participate in virtually every decision, became the norm. But children began to rebel in the 1990s against this excessive individualism. They developed new opinions as a counterbalance to the individualism. They thus came to value collective ties, such as faithfulness in a relationship, and "traditional" concepts such as family, to a greater degree than the generations before them.

The trend towards collectivism among the youth is little more than that. In their consumer choices they are still extremely individual; there is no question of a return to the neat consumer categories of times gone by. The "new collectivists" are ever more intangible for marketers.

Trend 3 *The breakthrough of the information society*

In the 1990s, there was a breakthrough of a whole range of information and communication technologies. One of the most important developments in this area was the arrival of the Internet. The breakthrough of the Internet resulted in the information explosion. Immediately afterwards came the incredible popularity of the mobile telephone. Young people seem to have little problem with the information explosion, and they can be contacted anywhere, at any time. They sms, surf, chat and phone as if their lives depend on it. The new information and communication technologies offer users an unprecedented ability to organize things. Networks and (virtual) communities spring up like mushrooms. Young people in particular make grateful use of the power they can exert thanks to these new technologies. These young people are not only very demanding and highly critical consumers, but also know exactly how to exert pressure on businesses.

Trend 4 *The information society comes of age*

After the arrival of the new millennium, the promises and expectations about the Internet were somewhat tempered. The Internet proved to be handy, sometimes indispensable, but on second thoughts seemed not to offer everybody the limitless possibilities that had initially been assigned to it. Internet companies in the 1990s had a golden future ahead of them; suddenly the sector was blighted with bankruptcies. Expectations about the Internet were also adjusted on a personal and social level. Constantly making new contacts and developing networks may be fun, but your home has to be pleasant as well. You can't live by the Internet alone. Thus the Internet is perceived by young people more realistically: it is handy, in certain areas very promising, but it is not a communications tool that makes everything else superfluous.

Trend 5 *Limits to world "makeability"*

The recent economic recession and the attacks of 11 September 2001 have made people realize that the world is not as "makeable" as once thought or hoped. The world cannot be steered by economic rationality and market thinking, and neo-liberalism does not, apparently, have the solution to every social problem. Young people react to this realization by intensifying their relationships with others. Within such relationships they can call on each other and reckon on help and support. Calculation is something people do as consumers; as people they are always there for friends and family.

Trend 6 *Call for norms and values*

In the 1990s, ideals and principles were still seen as awkward obstacles in reaching rational, pragmatic solutions; at the start of the 21st century, the need for norms and values increases. For years the individual held pride of place, but now there is a growing need for community. This expresses itself in a revaluation of traditional relationships, such as those with family and close friends. Clear statements and undiluted opinions are the new norm. Young people in particular value clear points of view, and suspect people who express themselves with excessive nuance of a lack of opinion. That people differ in their opinions is not a problem as long as there is mutual respect.

Trend 7 *Taking leave of limitless possibilities*

The 1990s were years of limitless possibilities. Everybody could succeed, if only they wanted to. Being successful was a choice. Now things are different. The right qualities are no longer a guarantee of a good job. The mood in the employment market is sombre. The realization is growing that we do not have our fate in our own hands. For young people, this doesn't however mean that they have adopted a fatalistic attitude to life.

Trend 8 *Diversity, religion and multiculturalism*

The blessings of the multicultural society are increasingly being questioned. European young people on the other hand have grown up in a multicultural society and do not know any different. They are less bothered by the unrest. Young people, both immigrant and indigenous, react to the diversity of culture by valuing their own culture much more strongly. Being proud of your roots is very important. What's more, the realization is growing that religion can be an important factor in developing a personality. Among young people especially, there is a growing interest in culture, religion and traditions. This does not mean that within ten years Europe will once again be religious in the old-fashioned sense, but religion will have returned as a player in the social arena.

Consequence 1 *Authenticity*

Authenticity is the key value in the life of young people. This implies more than simply doing your own thing. It means that you are "real", do not play games or act out a role. You show you are "real" by adopting clear standpoints. It is always better to have an un-nuanced standpoint than to have no standpoint at all. And artificial is completely unacceptable. This desire for authenticity also has consequences for the way young people act as consumers: something without a brand is better than a "dodgy" brand, namely the non-authentic, artificial brand. Authenticity is thus not only that to which young people aspire, it is also the standard against which other things are measured.

Consequence 2 *Individualism and collectiveness*

West European young people may be very individualistic in a number of areas, but in other areas they attach considerable value to stable connections. Young people see family connections as a contribution to their authentic identity, and not as a restriction on their freedom. For them, authentic life means entering into stable relationships and being prepared within them to make concessions if this is in the interests of the group. Today's young people have seen what a post-modern, ultra-individual life looks like and have decided that it is not for them. No freedom without constriction seems to be their motto.

Consequence 3 *From subculture to sub-club*

The time that a social preference, for example for music, automatically led to a "membership" of a pervasive subculture (and with it an avoidance of other subcultures) is over. The function of peer groups has thus been changed. Peers are no longer age contemporaries whom individuals need to copy as far as possible, but people with whom they can discuss opinions in a secure environment. People have an ongoing relationship with their peers, and there is no need to look like them. Thus the subculture – for so long the youth phenomenon *sine qua non* – is no longer so prevalent. Young people today are members of different sub-clubs, based on mutual interest, but it goes no further than that. Sub-clubs, unlike the former subcultures, do not determine the total personality of their members.

Consequence 4 *The faithful generation*

The appreciation of collective connections and the desire for authenticity have resulted in young people placing considerable value on faithfulness and loyalty in their most important relationships. They expect this faithfulness from anybody who aspires to have a relationship with them. This is not only true of individuals but also of companies.

Consequence 5 *High expectations and quality demands*

The young people of today grew up in a period when prosperity was high and continuing to rise. They are used to a high level of consumerism. They purchase a lot and their basic demand is for good quality in both products and services offered by a company. What's more, young people are highly autonomous consumers and do not allow their needs to be dictated to them.

Consequence 6 *Trust in the future*

Young people have a relatively high trust in the future. In the last few years, in which the world has become less stable, this is expressed in a "we're coming" attitude. Appealing to fear or distrust in the future makes no impression whatsoever on this generation.

Consequence 7 *Dealing differently with knowledge and information*

Thanks to the breakthrough of the information and communication society, young people are, from their earliest age, used to enormous amounts of information. They know that there is more information about any subject than a single individual can comprehend. Facts have to be analysed on the basis of limited knowledge. Young people are fully aware of this and it does not make them feel insecure. What's more, young people receive each day an enormous amount of images via television and other communication methods. They have grown up with this and are used to it. This means they are a highly visual generation.

Today's European youth are self-aware, place considerable value on authenticity, and are fully confident about their abilities and thus fairly optimistic about the future. Compared with previous generations, they are more relaxed and less rebellious. For marketers, however, they are not easily approached. Young people are self-willed, fully aware of the media, very critical, and used to the best. In addition, it is very difficult to place them in neat, recognizable subcultures with common and largely predictable preferences.

Young people in Eastern Europe have more opportunities than their contemporaries in the West; more about this in Megatrend 7. In the East, previous generations did not have the proper know-how, experience and attitude to pilot the countries through new times. Young people there reach for power much earlier. In the East, it is much more common to see people in their 20s and 30s becoming ministers or high-level civil servants, or leading business people. In the West, high positions are still held by baby-boomers and that makes it difficult for young people to obtain top positions of power: a tale of two worlds within one continent.

Conclusion

A combination of individualism and collectivism seems to lie ahead for Europe. Our consumer behaviour is something we decide for ourselves, but when it comes to social connections we seem to be group animals. We have high regard for family. We depend on our family members in times of adversity, and vice versa. Friends are also important in these uncertain times. We have the feeling that we must arm ourselves against "the enemy" and react together against established politics. Perhaps the clearest indication of this latter is the rejection of the European Constitution by France and the Netherlands, with the main reason, "We aren't satisfied with the way things are going right now." This is collectivism, in fact. But at the same time, we work more from home instead of going to the office and we cannot easily be fitted into neat consumer groups. This is individualism, in fact. And the fact that we can be quite comfortable with this dichotomy is shown by today's young people. The future is, after all, theirs.

Megatrend **5**
The New European perception of security

Introduction

Until recently, only a few European countries had anything to do with terrorist attacks. The IRA in the UK and ETA in Spain have been active for decades, but less so in recent years. Other countries have been temporarily plagued by terror. Examples are the Baader-Meinhof Group in Germany and the Red Brigades in Italy (both active in the 1970s). Then there are several small groups that are or have been active, such as the separatist movement in French Corsica and the Moluccan groups in the Netherlands. There have also been terrorist attacks committed in Europe by non-European terror organizations, such as the PLO during the Olympic Games in Munich in 1974 and the hijacking of the Italian cruise ship *Achille Lauro* in 1985. In the latter part of the 20th century, following the end of the Second World War, terror played an insignificant role.

In other areas of Europe, too, security was not an issue during the last few decades of the century. Security of hearth and home was relatively high. It was unnecessary for the middle classes and the elite to construct high fences around their properties, to hire body-guards (as protection against kidnapping and threats), install elaborate alarm systems and arrange other security measures in order to protect house and possessions. The crime figures were lower than in the United States, Brazil and India, where the rich take extensive precautions to protect themselves and their possessions. It is significant that the villas of the rich in Europe are in full view; in many South American countries, they are hidden behind walls and fences.

Petty crime in Europe was also relatively low. In the police states of Eastern Europe in communist times, there was little petty crime thanks to the strict social control and the police state. In Western Europe petty criminality was also restricted: pickpockets and muggings were limited in comparison with other non-European countries. Thanks to this, there was a very relaxed climate of fines and punishments. Criminals were kept in European "dolls' houses" and received relatively mild sentences for their misdemeanours. The justice system was feminized, not only in personnel (in 2005, the majority of people working in the justice system and the law were female), but also in attitude. Human rights and privacy legislation gained the upper hand, and it seemed that the rights of criminals were often considered more important than those of victims. The status of the justice system decreased. Privacy became more important than ever, even if this meant a decrease in the efficacy of the authorities.

Major criminal groups were active in Europe, and although they became more multinational and multicultural, they used Europe as a home base from which to organize their activities: gun-running, diamond smuggling, art thefts and smuggling, and other such matters. The policy seemed to be: make no waves and remain out of reach, and do your dirty work elsewhere. Because of this, much was tolerated in Europe.

Tolerance also applied to drugs. In various European countries, soft drugs were increasingly tolerated; in fact hard drugs were as well. That had an economic advantage, of course. Drug dealers invested a lot of their earnings from the "black" and "grey" economies in the "white" economy, such as real estate, car sales, the jewellery and watch trade, and clothing. And let us be honest: the majority of drugs were not imported into Europe for the starving junkies on the streets, but for the better-situated in various professions who may not have been addicted to drugs but nevertheless used them, for relaxation or to perform better in stressful professions.

But times change. At the start of the 21st century there is a new perception of security that is at times almost obsessive. This covers security in the broadest sense of the word: security in the home and garden, security on the streets, protection against multinational gangs, and against kidnapping and terror.

Trends in terror

The first trend that is clearly apparent is the "Israelization" of Europe. The terror attacks in Tel Aviv and other Israeli cities set the pattern for fundamentalist Islamic attacks in the streets of Madrid, London, Amsterdam and other European cities. This will lead to a period in which Europeans take leave of their open society and become more suspicious of each other and even more suspicious of outsiders and foreigners; governments will undertake more campaigns and other actions to alert the citizen to suspicious people, packages and so on. Awareness of terror increases. Since more use has to be made of the expertise of countries such as Israel and India, the image of these countries will improve throughout Europe.

In the time ahead, representatives of the Islamic terror move-ments will infiltrate relevant European organizations more and more efficiently. Such infiltrations will be increasingly undertaken by European converts to Islam, who do not have an Islamic appearance and can thus infiltrate them much easier. Conversely, the European security establishment will increasingly infiltrate

Islamic terror cells. This will be done by liberal Muslims who anticipate that a victory for Al Qaeda in Europe will result in a less liberal life for them.

Old and new terrorists will come together and cooperate with each other. There are strong indications that the attack in Madrid in 2004 was a joint venture between the Islamic Al Qaeda and the Spanish Basque ETA. More such collaborations are being forged: not only in Europe but also in South America, Al Qaeda works together with local terror groups related to the drugs trade. This form of globalization will increase in the near future, now that terror is primarily becoming nihilist by nature and less ideological.

"Terror education" is also becoming more global. Terror organizations need no longer set up training camps and education centres; the Internet offers increasing possibilities. It is easy to put the blueprints for making a bomb on the web, and ideological support is also taking place via the Internet.

Because of all this, privacy is becoming a thing of the past. More security cameras are appearing in streets, squares and other public places. Events, busy places in cities and public transport intersections are kept under surveillance more often and more intensively than ever. The cameras that used to be considered an intrusion of our privacy have become our friends, the equipment that safeguards our security. We become increasingly prepared to give up our privacy. We are prepared to have our bags and bodies searched at public events, museums and shopping centres, just as those people in countries where terror is commonplace have been accustomed to for so long.

The terrorist threats instigate new forms of xenophobia. Xenophobia used to be directed largely at foreigners; now it is aimed at Muslims. Europeans are becoming increasingly distrustful of people with a (perceived) Muslim appearance. The latter will feel this in job interviews, the body language of indigenous Europeans, and a cold shoulder from non-Islamic immigrants to Europe. This will also lead to greater difficulty for people from Islamic countries or with Islamic names to obtain visas and residence permits. In Mexico it is already the policy to refuse visas to people from Islamic countries. The expectation is that a similar policy will be adopted in Europe, although this may not be admitted publicly because of legal (anti-discrimination) considerations. The fear of Muslim terror will be translated into fear of Muslims in general, and investments by indigenous and non-Islamic immigrant Europeans will be concentrated in Muslim-free areas in and outside Europe.

A new apartheid will emerge. Muslims in European cities will increasingly live and work separately from non-Muslims. Separate development will result in less tension. Various groups of Muslims will leave Europe, but many indigenous Europeans will also leave what they consider a new battlefield. There will also be a decrease in the number of mixed marriages in Europe, thanks to the increasing xenophobia and the new nationalism.

Anti-Muslim sentiments will be expressed in the political arena. In Germany, the Netherlands, France and Belgium, parties with anti-Muslim policies are successful. In France, the Front National is doing well, even among Jewish voters who previously (when the party was also anti-Semitic) wanted nothing to do with it. The same is true of the Vlaams Belang (Flemish Interests) in Belgium. The Linkspartei (Left Party) in Germany is formally left-wing, but has adopted many of the anti-foreigner sentiments of the extreme right. In the German state Saxony, around 30 per cent of the vote is for the extreme right. In Denmark, the anti-immigration party has considerable voter support and participates in the government. In the UK, there is a market for anti-immigration parties. The Conservative Party made a play for this in the 2005 General Election.

As a response to Al Qaeda, terror groups will appear in Europe made up of indigenous Europeans – white terror groups – who direct their attacks primarily at Muslim targets in Europe. Until now these attacks have been isolated incidents, such as arson in mosques and Islamic schools and molesting Muslims (this was seen after the 2005 attacks in London), but in the coming years it is expected that some indigenous Europeans will organize themselves into terrorist groups that will attack Muslim and foreign buildings and locations within Europe in order to spread fear and intimidation. Their ultimate goal is to drive Muslims out of Europe.

In these periods of distrust for each other, we can expect mega-investments in security measures. Major investments will be made in security measures for harbours, airports, important buildings, public transport and major events, which might not necessarily increase security but will increase the perception of security. These will cost a lot of money and will thus be an attack on the economy – one of the most important targets of the terrorists. Causing economic exhaustion and fear syndromes is just as important as shedding blood.

There are more and more gadgets and technical gimmicks that claim to guarantee security. Some are for private individuals, others for professionals in the security industry. As we write this book, there are reports of trained flies and wasps that track down terrorists carrying bombs. But a new generation of bombs (of plastic rather than metal) will require new detection devices to replace metal detectors. The security branch can look forward to golden times.

Citizens will spend a lot of money on their security, in common with the United States where all self-respecting individuals have gas masks in their homes. Clothing will appear from materials that stop bullets and knives, as is currently found in Colombia and Israel. And do-it-yourself terrorist protection kits will appear, together with gas masks for civilians and water filters to counter the danger of water being poisoned.

The threat of terrorism has other consequences. Public transport for instance will suffer tremendously. Because of increasing terrorist attacks, fewer people will make use of it.

New forms of individual transport (one-person taxis in the form of bicycles or running on electricity) will emerge, in addition to regular taxis and part-time or full-time car ownership.

Sentences and new legislation will also become much harsher. Existing laws and rules will be eroded. There will be new laws that allow the deportation of hate-preaching imams and that restrict freedom of speech. There will be stiffer sentences, partly through US pressure, and later as a result of pressure from China and India. These future superpowers do not treat terrorists with kid gloves in their own countries and expect the same of their international partners. The other two BRIC countries, Brazil and Russia, are also not exactly gentle with people who disturb the (legal) peace.

Terror will also cause the demand for the reinstatement of the death penalty to become more insistent. Although this will do little to dissuade suicide bombers (who think that, at the moment of their death, they will be able to enjoy the pleasures of dozens of virgins), the law will appeal to the feelings of insecurity that exist among the population. Among the youth, there are already a large number who support the reintroduction of the death penalty. Among older people, particularly the baby-boomers, the majority are still against such a measure.

The emotions of groups within the population will be mobilized. Muslim media mobilize "fury" in Muslims for the suffering their fellow believers undergo in Chechnya, Kashmir, Sudan and Israel/Palestine, and call for a *jihad*, a holy war. In the confused Christian bloc, there will arise on the one hand a new religious revival as a response to this, and on the other atheists who become more and more convinced that they are right. They see religion as the opium of the people.

The "war on terror" will change slowly but surely into "negotiating terror". On the one hand there are an ever-growing number of security measures taken in the light of the war on terror; on the other, Europe is aware that it cannot win such a war and there will be (first privately, and then publicly) negotiations with Al Qaeda.

In order to give terror a proper place in our lives, it will be integrated into amusements, as happened earlier in our history. Many films were made about the war in Vietnam. The same is true of the Second World War. In Israel, there are comedies about Palestinian suicide bombers and there are countless jokes about them doing the rounds. Example: two vain Palestinian women, bombs concealed under their scarves and dresses, are waiting at a bus-stop in Tel Aviv. One says to the other: "Do I look fat in this dress?" In the future, we can expect Al Qaeda comedies, musicals and suchlike in Europe. Terror-entertainment will have arrived – *terrortainment.*

The creative industry and the security industry will increasingly join forces to combat terrorism. In the United States, after the attacks of 9/11, film writers from Hollywood were engaged by the security services to dramatize the terror. New collaborations arose between security experts and the creative industry, to allow them to get under the skin of the terrorists and put them a step ahead. In Europe, we can expect in the near future collaborations between the security industry and the creative industry. Novelists, game developers, (film) scriptwriters, film makers, playwrights, actors, fashion designers and others will increasingly contribute to the development of new security concepts. This new coalition is uniquely capable of "out of the box" thinking, and can thus combat the enemy in a creative and original way.

All these trends have one thing in common: they are all directly connected to the expectation that there will be more terrorist attacks in Europe. Cells of Muslim terrorists are spread throughout Europe (in the past age of naivety, they were formed in silence) and where the attacks will take place is anybody's guess.

A common security policy has been one of the pillars of the European Union since its foundation as the European Economic Community. The Organization for Security and Cooperation in Europe was founded in 1973. Now a European security coordinator has been named. The emphasis on security in Europe will only increase.

Terror scenarios

On 26 March 2004, after the appointment of Gijs de Vries as European security coordinator, the European ministers for home affairs and justice signed a Declaration on combating terrorism. The message of the Declaration is:

> The Union and its member states solemnly promise to do everything in their power to combat all forms of terrorism in accordance with the principles of the Union, the conditions in the manifesto of the United Nations, and the obligations accepted in 2001 with the adoption of resolution 1373 of the UN Security Council.

Since then cooperation between the various European security agencies has not structurally improved, even though this should have been the case. They exchange little or no information, scared that the information could find its way into the wrong hands. The trust between the various security services in Europe leaves a lot to be desired. For that reason, Europol is a paper tiger. There will need to be more attacks before security consciousness actually takes hold among the various stakeholders, for the risks are enormous. If attacks occur, they will most probably not be minor.

The US Department for Homeland Security has developed a number of disaster scenarios that could apply not only to the United States but also to Europe. The scenarios show that the "universal adversary" (UA) can attack in a variety of gruesome ways. And the big question is whether the European security services are a match for such duplicity. The second question that is raised is how far we will be capable of handling the consequences of the inevitable attacks. A major run on hospitals, the environmental effects of the attacks: we do not yet know the phenomenon well enough to prepare ourselves for it. The Department of Homeland Security works from the assumption that ten times as many people will rush to the hospital after an attack than is necessary, but that's a convenience figure that cannot be established accurately. When Al Qaeda attacked the Twin Towers on 9/11, the hospitals in New York were clogged up in no time, not with the wounded, but with the stream of people – 15 times more than those wounded – who went to hospitals demanding examinations because they had breathed in smoke. That had a paralyzing effect. The terrorists could not have asked for more. In Tokyo the effect was already well known. In 1995, members of the Aum Shinrikyo sect spread nerve gas through the metro system: not much, but enough to cause a rush on clinics that offered first-line medical treatment.

In 2004, President George W. Bush ordered that the consequences of such disasters be better identified, for it was clear that the United States did not have an answer to such disasters. The Department of Homeland Security developed 15 disaster scenarios which were published for a short time on the website of the Department of Defense in Hawaii. A telephone call from Europe alerted the mega-department in Washington, and on 16 March 2005 the National Planning Scenarios disappeared. But for a short time, it was possible to download information from this site.

The report did not predict where, when, or how Al Qaeda would strike; it calculated what would happen if an attack took place. It also calculated the consequences of a few natural disasters, such as a major earthquake, a hurricane or a flu pandemic. In addition, the document gave 12 examples of attacks. The report did not mention any terror group by name, but talked instead of the UA. What that adversary can do is terrifying, and can happen anywhere.

* The UA steals uranium in Russia and uses it to construct a nuclear bomb which is smuggled into the country. The

10 kiloton nuclear weapon is exploded in a business district. Everything is destroyed within a radius of one kilometre. Flying debris causes thousands of casualties and damage in a radius of six kilometres. Electrical appliances in the city no longer work because of the electromagnetic shock wave. Almost half a million people run through the streets, and the effects of the radiation and fall-out are felt to a distance of 250 kilometres. An area of 8000 square kilometres has to be cleaned up, something that costs billions of dollars. The economy is hit hard; it will take years for the country to get back on its feet.

- The UA drives a lorry through five cities and spreads clouds of anthrax. After a couple of days, spleen fever breaks out and the hospitals are overrun. Problems arise because the symptoms are not recognized instantly, and medications run out. The population is alarmed and pharmacists are terrorized. About 300,000 people are infected; 13,000 do not survive.

- The UA succeeds in releasing the plague virus in three places simultaneously: a railway station, the toilets in a large airport, and a sports stadium. The operation only takes a few hours. Within three days the disease has crossed the ocean, carried by travellers. A day later 11 countries raise the alarm, following the United States and Canada. Then 8000 people die. The fear among the population keeps people locked away in their homes; banks, offices and factories collapse. A few weeks later – and after a further 2500 deaths – life gradually returns to normal. But the traumas and invalids remain.

- The UA flies an advertising plane over a major football stadium and for five minutes sprays a mixture of mustard gas and Lewisite into the air. The spectators experience respiratory problems and flee in panic. There are more than 150 casualties; 1000 people have to be treated. Many of them suffer from permanent lung damage and blindness; the mustard gas can also cause cancer. The damage (destruction, detoxification) amounts to half a billion dollars.

- After two years of preparation, the UA lands helicopters in the grounds of a major oil refinery, launches rockets at the oil tanks, and places several explosives. Two nearby oil tankers are attacked, catch fire and sink. It takes days to put out the fires. Downwind, panic breaks out among the population. A few hundred people die as a result of poisonous fumes and accidents; the hospitals are full to overflowing. 700,000 people lose their homes. The economic damage runs into many billions.
- The UA releases the nerve gas sarin in three places into the ventilation systems of large apartment buildings (20 floors, 2000 people) in a major city. The terrorists have taken six months to prepare this attack, which takes just ten minutes to carry out. There are 6000 deaths, largely among the tenants, but also among the emergency services, because the gas is odourless and works quickly. The panic will be great; the direct economic damage runs into the hundreds of millions of dollars.
- The UA explodes a bomb in an industrial area near a tank of liquid chloride. Downwind, panic takes hold of the population. The chloride gas that is released is poisonous and causes 17,500 deaths and tens of thousands of serious injuries. Nearly half a million people rush to the hospitals for treatment. There are also casualties in the resulting traffic chaos. It takes weeks to restore order.
- The UA makes "dirty bombs" from dynamite and the radioactive caesium-137. It can pick up the components anywhere. The bombs are exploded in three medium-sized cities. The areas within a few kilometres of the explosions are contaminated with fall-out. The dust also penetrates the metro system and large buildings through their ventilation systems. Fires break out, caused by burst gas pipes. The explosions cause relatively little damage: 36 housing blocks are severely damaged,

180 people die in each city, but the panic is terrible. The material damage is enormous because large sections of the city have to be demolished, decontaminated and rebuilt. It takes years before the cities are once again fully functional.

- There are simultaneous bomb attacks on various targets. The UA explodes car bombs and several improvised bombs in a sports arena and its underground parking garage. A few suicide bombers take care of the metro system. When the transportation of the wounded gets underway, a large car bomb is exploded near the entrance to the major hospital. To disrupt the rescue efforts even further, the terrorists use an ambulance for one of their bombs. The chaos and terror is enormous. Around 100 people die.
- The UA carries out an attack on a meat factory and a processing plant for orange juice. Meat and juice are contaminated with liquid anthrax by terrorists who are employed in the factories through local temporary employment agencies. The anthrax spreads rapidly throughout the country via the distribution networks. 300 people die, a far greater number become

ill, and thousands of people rush to the hospitals for check-ups. The meat and juice industries collapse, and the fear virus affects everybody else in the food industry.

- Spies working for the UA select suitable cattle markets and livestock haulers as targets for spreading foot and mouth virus; the virus spreads rapidly throughout the country. The terrorists are not concerned so much with causing human casualties, as with causing disruption and economic damage. The greater the area of infection, the greater the problems caused by transport restrictions, the culling of livestock, and the resistance to controls. The public is afraid of eating steak, the export of meat stops, and the damage runs into the hundreds of millions. It takes months before the mouth and foot crisis is under control.

- The UA succeeds in letting a number of hackers make a cyber attack on a number of vital computers. Millions of credit cards become worthless, or are misused because the PIN codes are deciphered. Cash registers and giro systems are unusable, if only because the public no longer has any faith in them. Salaries are not paid on time, foreign speculators no longer trust the US dollar, and the financial markets are plunged into crisis.

Homeland Security was not concerned with listing all the possible risks. Plane hijacking is not mentioned, because terrorists have done this so often it has been replayed countless times. Some attacks in the report cause human casualties, others cause economic damage. Some, despite all the suffering, are local; others spread them themselves rapidly. All the scenarios, however, have one thing in common: the enormous disruption that follows. Panic, hospitals overwhelmed with wounded and people who want to be examined as a precaution, and loss of consumer confidence can completely paralyze a society. Terrorists know that. And we know that terrorists know that. That causes a general feeling of unease in Europe. In fact, that's putting it rather mildly. We are scared: we feel unsafe in our own continent, in our own country, city, neighbourhood. And that will not improve during the coming decades.

All this changes matters about war and security, says the Israeli security specialist Martin Van Creveld in his book *The Transformation of War*. He predicts that major wars will slowly but surely belong to the past, and be replaced by what he calls LICs: low-intensity conflicts. These will take the place of wars in which states fight against states. In such wars, the cost of human lives is enormous. During the Second World War 30,000 people died every day – and that for six long years. Compare that with the nearly 3000 deaths in the WTC attack in New York on 9/11 – it's peanuts.

Van Creveld studied 3000 years of war history, from the Sumerians to the present day. In his opinion, terrorism is ancient. A characteristic of terrorist attacks is that small commando units can cause enormous damage. The price–performance ratio is extremely favourable. Battles in which enormous armies face each other are a relatively recent occurrence. But with the erosion of the modern state, we are witnessing a rediscovery of ways of waging war – for example, those that reached their peak in the Middle Ages – that have since been forgotten: deception, betrayal, ambush, anarchy and all kinds of terrorism. According to Van Creveld, it no longer makes sense in this century to invest large sums in classic war material. He writes, "We must fight terrorism with the weapons of terrorism."

If you want to fight terrorism efficiently you must, according to him, train proficient commando units who can penetrate to the core of the enemy, attack swiftly and disappear again. Security services will become increasingly important, and will concern themselves increasingly with our private lives. In exchange for safety, civilians will have to give up some of their freedom and privacy. The Middle Ages are returning. At that time, the feudal state was based on barter trade: the lords offered protection in exchange for a part of the harvest. That is now returning, albeit in a modern guise. In countries such as Somalia, it is already the case: the warlords have taken over this task from the state and are lords and masters in their own limited zone.

The whole security business has thus taken off thanks to this. Security is a commodity, a raw material that has to be purchased with hard cash. Citizens will have to take care of their own security, or will have to pay a lot for it. Van Creveld believes that terror and anarchy will become commonplace; we will have to learn to live with them. He prefers that situation above major conflicts between states, which have always cost a greater many more lives. He despises the state, which according to him is a monster that fortunately does not have a long life ahead of it. In his book he writes, "War is the soul of man, written in large letters." That is a metaphor that is taken from Plato. War is, according to him, the naked human soul in its most extreme, its most sublime, but also its most terrible form.

For Von Clausewitz, war is a matter of politics, but Van Creveld thinks about words such as pride, games, the pure desire to win. Etymologically, the word "war" actually means play. Chil-

dren play at war. Adults also in fact do that, in their cruellest, most sublime, most authoritative and also most terrible way. Van Creveld comments, "Just look carefully at the way Palestinian boys throw stones at Israeli soldiers: There is a lot more sport and games about it than you think." About Islam in Europe he says:

I know very tolerant Muslims, even here in Israel: people who are opposed to all forms of violence, genuine pacifists. I know Muslims who are rightly indignant about the WTC attack. In itself, Islam is tolerant – I do not know any other religion that intrinsically contains such a love of peace. But in the situation that exists today, I would not wish to live in any Islamic country, either as Jew or Christian.

Gated communities and cocooning

We have discussed security at a macro level, but the theme is also relevant at a micro level, the level of the household. A clear result is the growth market that European project developers are experiencing for various forms of gated communities. These are (protected) housing estates or flats, where people live with "people of their own kind". Ethnic or socioeconomic diversity is not desirable, for this only causes unrest. There is maximum security in the area, including surveillance cameras, alarm installations and guard duty by security companies. While people stay in their own gated community, they do not have to worry about their safety or that of their children and property. Theft, burglary, muggings and possible attacks belong to the past.

Apparently more and more people think there is money to be made from such a concept. In fact, some apartment buildings are already gated communities, and this concept of protected living will take on large proportions in the future. That is partly a result of "part-time living". Because people live in several places at once, it is important that their houses and possessions are safe when they are elsewhere. They will therefore invest more in new security equipment, surveillance cameras, all types of (silent) alarms, neighbourhood watches and private security officers. In France there are small companies that take care of the maintenance and security of holiday homes belonging to North Europeans who live there part time. These houses are frequently a target for burglars.

The enthusiasm for gated communities is large among the prosperous classes, and it will not be long before the concept is common in European cities. If Islam increases and Western Europe becomes part of Eurabia, it will become a must for those who have not left for New Europe. Little can happen to people at home in their own fort, and all that security equipment will give a feeling of safety. A good example of this is an extra-secure room in the house where residents can go if thieves break in. The thief cannot get to them while they are in there, and they can use a dedicated telephone to call for help, and make use of emergency food rations and lighting in the event of having to stay there for a longer time.

New technology is being used to give apprehensive civilians a (greater) feeling of security in and around their houses. Because most casualties in a bomb attack are caused by flying glass, windows will be covered with a special foil which ensures that if the glass is shattered for any reason, it does not fly around, but remains stuck to the foil and simply crumbles. Seniors, who are traditionally more easily scared than young people, will stimulate the demand for new security concepts and equipment. Very soon, you will be able to buy security equipment at the supermarket. Security-conscious seniors can form virtual communities and warn each other if there are problems, a form of grey power.

Cocooning will increase, particularly among seniors. If, in the perception of citizens, it is so unsafe outside, it is better to seek entertainment at home. People will make fewer visits to the cinema, and instead download films from Internet and enjoy them at home while cameras keep their eyes on doors and windows, security systems safeguard them and their property, and a security guard in the lobby prevents hooligans from getting in.

Because of the feelings of insecurity, cash will become less common. In countries with high levels of insecurity, such as Brazil, you can even purchase a tube of toothpaste costing 1 with a credit card. ATMs in Brazil, and also in India, Indonesia and South Africa, are generally guarded by armed security employees of the bank. In Europe, payment by credit card, PIN direct debit card, and other plastic payment methods will increase as a response to the feelings of insecurity. For seniors, there are already ATMs inside banks; you need a card to get in. New identification methods and new ways of protecting credit cards and direct debit cards will replace the PIN, partly with forgetful seniors in mind. Iris scans and fingerprints are obvious choices. In places where people feel at greater danger than elsewhere – for example, at ATMs in very busy or perhaps even very deserted points in big cities – there will be increased security, with either cameras or live personnel.

Private security will increase; the role of the police will decrease. To turn European countries into police states is costly and extremely labour-intensive, as was shown by the Eastern bloc countries during communist times. Ageing and a reduction in the population will decrease the labour pool in Europe in the coming years, but technology offers possibilities for new types of security. Armies and police forces will not grow larger in years to come. We can expect, however, a growth in European intelligence services. Private security firms will also increase. In Germany, the Netherlands and various other European countries, more people are employed by private security firms than by the police; the same is true in India. There will be an ongoing growth in the market for bodyguards. The elite and upper middle classes will make use of them. Job integration will also increase. Professional chauffeurs to anyone who is anyone will receive training in how to get the car and its occupants to safety if there is a kidnapping threat, and how to react to gun shots being fired at the car.

Identification will become more and more important, and the technical possibilities will also grow in number. In many European countries there is already an identification obligation, and until now identification cards have been sufficient. But the biometric passport is coming, and iris scans are already being used.

Car theft will also become a thing of the past. The GPS systems and car tracking systems that are already available make it possible to follow and track down stolen cars. New identification systems will ensure that every car part is numbered and marked, and thus stealing cars and breaking them down in order to sell the parts throughout Europe will also be a crime of the past. For the European elite, there will be a growing number of armoured cars on the market. In the future, the use of new materials will make these lighter and thus less fuel-consuming than the current generation of armoured vehicles.

Bullet-proof fabrics are also appearing. As we already mentioned, recent fashion shows in Colombia and Israel included a new generation of fabric that is bullet-proof but looks just like cotton. A summer dress that looks as if it is made of muslin and is nevertheless bullet-proof will be available soon in Europe. Clothing that offers safety is appearing. Since there will be an increasing use of plastics, natural materials (like fur and silk) will be used much more for accessories (scarves, fur collars, fur hats), and this will allow someone to be both a well-protected city girl and a "back-to-nature" country girl at the same time. This will mean real fur instead of fake fur, and real silk instead of artificial silk.

People want to spend less time walking in the street. In the perception of the European citizen in the 21st century, it is dangerous to walk on the streets of a city. They believe they can only go out on the streets if they are armed to the teeth in order to protect themselves from danger. An increasing number of women will carry pepper sprays with them in order to shake off attackers, even though it is legally prohibited in some countries. New ways of frightening off or disabling attackers are now being developed and will soon appear on the market. The mobile telephone, the GSM, is also a security weapon. You can use it to sound the alarm if danger occurs (the new generation of GSMs will include this facility). The camera built in to the GSM is useful for photographing thieves, attackers and so on, and this will eventually allow them to be identified and apprehended. Nevertheless, tomorrow's citizen will want to walk less, and therefore will want to park near to his or her destination. Solutions are also coming for this, partly made possible by the reduction in the number of people living in Europe. Fewer people will live here in the future, and this will make room for parking facilities.

Security gurus will achieve the status of pop stars in Europe. They will gain in stature, become media stars, will be frequent guests on talk shows. They will have their own programmes on radio, television and the Internet, will write regular columns in newspapers, and their weblogs will attract many visitors. Some security gurus will get on even better and perhaps make the transition into politics. They offer the electorate a certain feeling of security, and that makes them attractive as politicians. This has happened in the past – General Eisenhower became president of the United States and General de Gaulle president of France. In the near future, it is not completely unthinkable that security gurus (from the police, military or security agencies) will become political leaders.

It will naturally make a big difference if the rapidly progressing gene technology succeeds in eliminating the gene that causes criminal behaviour. How wonderful it would be to implant in the brains of every criminal a chip that prevents any criminal impulse being passed on to the body. Just imagine: Your brain thinks about robbing a little old lady of her handbag. Before you can put this into action, the chip springs into action. Stop! Don't do it! It's not your handbag; help the lady across the road, you naughty boy! And obediently you follow the new orders that have been issued by your chip-manipulated brain. People are seriously brainstorming about such possibilities in think-tanks made up of psychiatrists, criminologists, gene technologists and people from the industry.

Major non-terrorist criminality

Major criminality will also increase in 21st-century Europe. The following trends can be identified.

The number of multinational gangs will increase. Roma networks will emerge, largely in Eastern Europe, and will join up with the Roma networks that have long existed in Western Europe. Serbs and Chechens will also have important functions in these networks. This cross-border collaboration will result in successful criminality with PIN cards, debit cards and credit cards; this is already largely dominated by the Roma.

Drugs will largely be legalized and major users will increasingly be spared from prosecution. Many drugs – cocaine, for example, and Ecstasy – are used in Europe by people from the higher classes who are generally able to deal with them. They pay good money for them, which is one of the reasons this industry will continue. There is something to be said for legalizing drugs in Europe, as is already the case with alcohol, but a tolerance policy is much more likely. The drugs business is lucrative and will remain so, and it will not be prosecuted as aggressively as it should be (not least, because drugs provide a

source of finance for Al Qaeda), because much attention is directed at fighting terrorism.

Black and white economies will increasingly coexist and intermingle. Income from drugs and other regular criminal activities is traditionally ploughed back into the regular economy. In Europe, that has always happened with some discretion; it does so less openly than in a country such as India, where in the Bollywood film scene legal and criminal funds go hand in hand. Films are financed simultaneously by criminal and professional film financiers. Extortion of the rich is prevalent, something that until now has been limited in Europe. In the future, globalization will also strike in this area. Asians from emerging economies who are facing extortion or blackmail in their own countries, will settle in Europe – either part-time or full-time – and will, in turn, be bothered here by their much-travelled criminal persecutors. Bribery and corruption will also infiltrate European business transactions.

Major crime networks will increasingly finance terror. Up until now various forms of criminality such as the drugs trade (with the exception of Colombia, where there are links between drug dealers and terrorists) have had no links with terror organizations. They were independent. This was also true of those who copied designer clothes and other luxury items: it was big business in the European market, where many top brands in the field of fashion and cosmetic originate. They are increasingly the victim of counterfeiting, and increasingly the counterfeit organizations are allied with Al Qaeda.

The so-called hawala banking system is nearing its end. This centuries-old form of banking which originated in India has had its best days in Europe. It is a form of cash money transfer that can only too easily be used for criminal ends.

Border controls will return. Border control has been abolished between the Schengen countries in Europe, but it will be reintroduced, as a result of the new thinking about security and fear management. The arrival of asylum seekers will increasingly be obstructed. Ideas from places such as Libya to create a European asylum-seekers centre there will win support. Human rights will be made subservient to security. There will come an end to the exaggerated rights of criminals and detainees.

One can expect that, if European governments prove incapable – or insufficiently capable – of guaranteeing the security of their citizens, "warlords" or private anti-terror units will emerge, as has happened in other countries. In India, police often shoot and kill many criminals (murderers, drug dealers, extortionists, blackmailers, kidnappers, terrorists) during "encounters". That the death penalty formally does not exist in India is a detail; only idiots bother about that. The death penalty does in fact exist; it is carried out by the Indian police, without intervention from a judge. The CIA does the same, and so too does the Israeli Mossad. Groups of Brazilian police agents operate "off duty" as "death squads", without this resulting in lawlessness and lack of justice. In Europe, we do not yet know this phenomenon, but we will be confronted by it in the 21st century.

Conclusion

In Western European countries, where the conflict between Christianity and Islam will take place, I see a transitional period in which various security enclaves coexist, perhaps separated by physical walls or secured in some other way. In Europe, fear management will have increasing sway. Because traditional criminality (the drug trade, counterfeiting) will have links with international Muslim terror, and because traditional European terror organizations such as ETA will join forces with Al Qaeda, security will be a more important issue than ever. We no longer feel safe in our own places of residence, and in the long term we shall shut ourselves off from these dangers by turning our homes into forts. Will we ever break free of this spiral? Partly yes, partly no. If Eurabia becomes a fact, then in that part of Europe, this phenomenon will be stronger than ever. In New Europe, however, these feelings will be less of a concern. The obsession with security will continue to manifest itself in the western part of Europe. Twenty-first-century Europe will be characterized by living in a world of identification chips, security agents and electronic surveillance cameras. The right to privacy will hardly exist: it is far too dangerous. The security industry can look forward to golden times.

Megatrend **6**
From the Argentinean model to the New European model

Introduction

Until the Second World War, Argentina was one of the eight richest countries in the world. It exported grain, hides and meat, and used the income from these to develop industry. But things went wrong in the 1950s. Argentina faced competition from cheaper agricultural countries, and its industry had not yet reached a level that would allow it to compete with other industrialized countries. Under the leadership of the presidential couple Juan and Eva Peron, the economy was not modernized; on the contrary, the structural causes of the malaise were allowed to continue: high inflation, low productivity, low exports, share speculation by the elite, and enormous government spending (for example, on the extensive welfare state). The national debt grew and grew because Argentina continued borrowing from other countries. It was only later, under President Alfonsin, that something was done: Argentina received aid from the IMF, the Argentinean currency was coupled to the US dollar, and government spending was curbed. But the consequence was that the income the population had to spend fell and the economy stagnated. In 2002 the crisis reached a head: we all remember pictures of the long queues in front of Argentinean banks. In 2003 there was some improvement. But Argentina is not exactly one of the world's most prosperous countries – quite the opposite, in fact.

It looks as if Europe could be set on the same path. Europe runs the risk of being overtaken by the new superpowers. It no longer excels as it did. The majority of new inventions come from other continents, America and especially Asia. An increasing number of scientists and students leave Europe and work or study at better universities elsewhere, for example in the United States and China. In the top 40 universities in the world – the Jiao Tong University in Shanghai produces such a list every so often – there are only six European universities, of which four are in the UK, one in Zurich, and one in the Netherlands (the University of Utrecht occupies the 40th place). Every year, more engineers graduate from Indian universities than from all European universities together in ten years. Decades of prosperity have made Europe lazy and soft. Here, too, we have an extensive welfare state. We seem to be rushing headlong into the Argentinean model: an economic decline that is virtually irreversible. Or, as the Dutch Minister of Foreign Affairs, Ben Bot, said so succinctly in a lecture he gave in The Hague on 14 February 2005, "If beautiful Europe doesn't wake up, she is in danger of being kidnapped once more – not this time by Zeus disguised as an ox, but by an Asian tiger." In that same lecture he said, "A combination of Asian industry and European passiveness will irreversibly result in employment and high-value knowledge being sucked out of Europe."

People in the European Union have been aware of this for some time, and have tried to tackle the problem in the Lisbon agenda, which states: "Europe must become the most competitive and dynamic knowledge economy in the world, in which sustainable economic growth leads to more and better jobs and a more cohesive society." This aim was formulated during the European Council in Lisbon in March 2000 and has since been known as the Lisbon strategy. By 2010, the European economy must be the most competitive in the world. The treaty states that every European country should spend at least 3 per cent of its gross national product on R&D. The European Commission publishes an annual report in which the progress made by the various European member states on the Lisbon agenda is measured. It looks at education performance, research expenditure and employment productivity.

The Lisbon agenda in 2005

In 2005 – five years after the framing of the Lisbon agenda and halfway towards 2010 – it doesn't look likely that the aims will be achieved. According to Frits Bolkestein, a former European Commissioner, this is largely the fault of the "old" European countries, Germany and France:

> The reforms they will have to undertake in the labour market are painful, and they are not prepared to make them. Because of the stability pact, devaluation is no longer possible and so the only possibilities that remain are macroeconomic structural reforms in the real economy, such as a lower growth in wages. The population protests against such measures and governments don't like that.

This was sufficiently known beforehand, is Bolkestein's opinion:

> When the Lisbon agenda was framed it was clear that it could never be achieved; people didn't realize what they were saying. Europe can never become more competitive than the United States; nevertheless, it is vital that Europe's competitive position becomes stronger.

A reduction in the welfare state is essential in this, says Bolkestein:

> In Scandinavian countries, governments are doing very well
> in this area. They do not have a policy of tolerance there. If
> you are not ill then you just have to work and you do not
> receive any benefits. The taxes are higher and the knowledge
> economy is growing faster there than in the rest of Western
> Europe. In Western Europe, people – particularly the baby-
> boomers – have become spoiled.

The lack of action directed at a strong European economy could
have something to do with the European mentality – or rather, the
West European mentality. The Americans have their "American
dream", an ideal that every American strives after. That ideal is for
economic prosperity and personal happiness through hard work,
and so to push the country forward thanks to the efforts of its
people. Nationalism plays an important role in this. We earlier
concluded that nationalism is not doing very well in Europe; in
some countries it is not present at a national level, let alone that
Europeans are not at all nationalistic about their continent. In
America, people live to work; in Europe we work to live. Money
here is something dirty; in America they love it.

   A European dream would be a wonderful motivator for the European economy. Hands together and go for it. The idea of a European
dream was thought up by the American Jeremy Rifkin, president of
the Foundation of Economic Trends in Washington, and one of the
most controversial economists in the world. Rifkin's books include
The End of Work (1995), *The Biotech Century* (1998), *The Age of Access*
(2000) and *The Hydrogen Economy* (2002). In 2004 he published *The
European Dream*. Jeremy Rifkin is adamant: "Europe must dare to
believe in its own dream." Europe has a dream, he says, and on many
points it is much more suitable for today's world than the American
dream. Americans are concerned about money; the European dream
is about solidarity, sustainability, human rights. Rifkin says:

The European dream is about involvement of people. That means: not leaving everybody at the mercy of the market, respecting diversity (even though you are much too afraid of immigrants), quality of life for society, sustainable development of the planet, social rights and universal human rights, and peace.

We shouldn't trade in this dream for a capitalist society such as America, Rifkin adds. Dismantling the welfare state means – to put it simply – a reduction in purchasing power which leads to a fall in spending and an economy that no longer grows. The problem, according to Rifkin, does not lie in the welfare state. What should we then do? "Europe has a golden goose that is hardly being fed," says Rifkin:

The alternative model for the bankrupt American model that is sighing under a burden of debt is the integration of potentially the richest internal market in the world, from the Irish Sea to the doorstep of Russia: 455 million consumers .... This is what Europe must do. Within fifteen years, there has to be an integrated communication, energy, and transport network for the whole Union. Within ten years, there should be one set of rules for trade and labour. English should, in ten years time, become the *lingua franca* of the business world. That doesn't solve all the problems. The fear for immigration has to be overcome, because there are many more immigrants and many more children required to prevent Europe from becoming an old-age pensioners' home. But in this way, you give yourself a few years extra for building a sustainable economy, to think about the role of work and all the other consequences of globalisation, and to create a new energy system based on hydrogen.

This new mentality can be seen in Eastern Europe, says Frits Bolkestein:

Eastern Europe is much more market-oriented. Before the ten new member states joined the European Union on 1 May 2004, I visited every one of them. The progress was tangible. The Czech Republic and Croatia are doing very well. They are moving ahead faster than the rest, undoubtedly influenced by the former Austro-Hungarian culture, of which they were formerly a part. Estonia is doing well – people are really committed there. The governments in all these countries enjoy the support of the population. The Prime Minister of Slovenia said to me: "We have little solidarity here and considerable motivation." That's the way it's working there now. We don't understand that in Western Europe. I was also very impressed by the young people, particularly the young women. They have enormous motivation to perform well. You really can talk about a new Europe and an old Europe. In the new Europe, things are going so well that many East European emigrants are returning from America. There are now indications of a reverse brain-drain in Eastern Europe, and many highly trained people can find work in their home countries. By the way, I would also consider Great Britain a part of new Europe; things there are going extremely well indeed.

Eastern Europe

The countries of Eastern Europe can be divided into a number of different categories. Tom Kuperus, a specialist on Eastern Europe, categorizes them as follows:

- Baltic states. Their cultures have considerable similarities to the Scandinavian cultures. Religion is less important.
- Russia. European in population and culture, but the majority of the country is geographically part of Asia.
- The former European communist countries. These are

countries such as White Russia, Ukraine and Moldavia. They generally have a rather "rough" culture, underworld and normal society are closer than anywhere else, and there are many "weekend warriors". Religion is important there. There are more nomadic cultures.

- Visegrad countries: Poland, Hungary, the Czech Republic and so on. They used to be part of the Austro-Hungarian double monarchy, which was in fact a predecessor of the European Union, and as such they are more accustomed to the European way of working and thinking. People here talk Indo-European languages. Religion is less important.
- Northern Balkan countries: Romania, Bulgaria, Croatia. In culture, closer to "old Europe," with long traditions in business, cultural exchange, and so on with the rest of Europe. Religion is less important.
- Southern Balkan countries: Albania, Serbia and so on. These are farther from the centre of Europe, culturally somewhat "rougher" than other European countries, and frequently have an anti-modernistic view of the world. Religion is important. Less densely populated.

Despite these differences, it is possible to distil a number of trends for Eastern Europe. Through research, our own observations, and discussions with leading Eastern European specialists such as Frits Bolkestein, Caroline van Thessen, Karin Veldman and Tom Kuperus, the following trends have emerged:

- Less freedom of movement for people. The past centuries have seen various population groups spreading out to places outside their original homeland. The integration of all these minorities results in considerable ethnic-cultural tension. Because of this, there will, in the future, be less freedom of movement in these countries, is the opinion of European expert Caroline van Thessen.

- EU norms, even for non-EU countries. Trading with the EU will be harmonized according to EU norms, even for those countries that have not (yet) joined the EU, is the expectation of Eastern European expert Karin Veldman.

- Politics, enlightened thinking and progressive ideology will become more religious. Traditional and new religious forms will reach for power after being suppressed by communism. This doesn't necessarily result in full churches, but certainly anti-Islam feelings will increase. People don't want to experience what has happened in Western Europe.

- Orientation towards America. Eastern Europeans will increasingly orientate themselves towards the United States. Students will go to study in the United States rather than in Western Europe. Militarily and ideologically, there will also be an orientation towards the United States, partly through the large immigrant communities that live in the United States. These bicultural tribes will perform a bridge function with Eastern Europe. The United States will also invest more in the East.

- Israelization of Eastern Europe. Investments by Jews (whether or not of Eastern European origin) from Israel, the United States and Western Europe will increase. Israelis will move there either temporarily or permanently. Israeli security concepts will be applied and people will try to prevent the arrival/growth of Muslim populations.

- Generation struggle. Young people, often with Western educations, will seize power; older people, often with a Stalinist background, will be pushed to one side. A restricted welfare state, few provisions for the elderly. And that will remain so, despite increasing social unrest.

- Increasing nationalism. That was always strong, but it will increase, in the diasporas as well.

- Criminal environments will become more like salons. Criminal money will be used to acquire companies, and the underworld will come out into the light. Vague divisions.

- New answers to modernity. Modernity and globalization are unattractive for many people from the lower classes. This can cause unrest in Western Europe, from which the Eastern European countries can learn a lot. There is currently too little attention paid to this theme, but this will change.
- Prevention of the creation of the welfare state. That has a communist ring about it, and people see the misery it has caused in the West. In Eastern Europe, traditional societies will be created with a market economy in line with the American model. Gay marriage will, I think, not arrive quickly in the East. Raw capitalism which includes elements that we in the West find difficult to accept (such as the flat tax). Before things get better, they will get worse.
- Weak states, strong social middle field. The government is still weak, and will become gradually stronger in the coming time, but not as strong as in the West. The population will arrange their affairs and business deals in various collectives. Ex-communists will remain a power factor.
- Historical awareness. Knowledge of one's own history is important and will become even more so.

The city of Vienna will play an important role in the dialogue between east and west. The city has a strategic position, at the heart of the former Danube monarchy, and has had to deal with invaders and occupiers from both East and West. Its position between the East and the West is also geographically beneficial. In the coming time, many international affairs between East and West will be organized from Vienna. Young people who have a high level of ambition in the East will play a crucial role, as we shall see in the next megatrend.

Until now, it has largely been Americans, Germans, Dutch, Austrians, Brits and Swedes who are active in the East. This will change in the future: South European countries will also become active in the East.

Old and New Europe in the 21st century

Gerald Scharrer

There is an old and there is a new Europe. The new Europe is emerging in Central and Eastern Europe, more or less on the foundations of the old Austro–Hungarian monarchy. For me, as an Austrian, this is a very interesting time. Vienna, a city too big for such a small country as Austria, is booming nowadays with business enterprises aimed at the East. Trading with Eastern Europe, developing new projects in Eastern Europe: it all makes sense in the new Vienna, almost a century after the collapse of the old Austro–Hungarian monarchy. In a way this monarchy was the precursor of the European Union. It was a union of states, cooperating more or less like the current European Union. The monarchy fell apart as a result of nationalism. I hope this won't be the case with the European Union, now that nationalism is rising all over Europe.

I myself enjoy these times in history, in my opinion the best time in history ever. I live most of the time in sunny Spain, can pay in euros almost everywhere in Europe, and my business life is spread over several European countries at the same time. The future of a more united Europe seems inspiring enough to me. Yet I recognize the differences between old and new Europe, since I'm part of both of them.

In Eastern Europe I sense that the people take the United States more as their reference point than Western Europe. They prefer their children to study in the United States, not in Western Europe. Most Western European countries are hardly visible in the East. I hardly see Italians, Spaniards or other people operating in Eastern Europe, while the Swedish, the Germans and the Austrians are there, as are the Americans.

In a way the new Europe is also the new America. Many investors come from the States, sometimes with East European roots (their forefathers migrated to the United States long ago).

More and more come from Israel (also often with East European roots). US media such as CNN pay lots of attention to the East, much more than Western European media.

The old Europe is fading away. No new ideas, new energy, new masterworks of art, no new scientific or other achievements originate there. They come from the East now and will do for the rest of the 21st century, with Vienna as the booming centre. But until the bomb falls in Western Europe I'll stay in sunny Spain. Vienna may be beautiful, but the winters are too cold.

Gerald Scharrer, from Austria, owns publishing companies in Spain and the Canary Islands, his current residence. He is also working in international tourism marketing and on creating business relationships between China, Eastern Europe and Central Europe for the Canary Islands.

New economic pillars for Europe

In 21st-century Europe, there is enough economic activity to be developed. This will have to be unique and contemporary. It is ridiculous to believe that Europe can surpass America and Asia. The world's most competitive economy in the 21st century will not be located in Europe, but that's not necessary. Europe can earn money from a number of unique economic pillars, and the expectation is that it will develop these. The most important economic pillars for the new Europe are reviewed here.

Pillar 1 *Tourism*

In 2003, the European Commission wrote the following to the European Parliament:

Guaranteeing sustainable European tourism in economic,

social and environmental areas is essential as a contribution to sustainable development in Europe and in the world, but also for the viability, healthy growth, the competitive position, and the commercial success of this very important economic sector. The challenges for a sustainable European tourism lie both in the area of consumption patterns and in the area of production patterns, in other words the value chain and the tourist destinations. In order to break through the non-sustainable patterns in the tourist sector, sustainable behaviour from tourists and good governance from governments and corporate life are crucial.

("Basic guidelines for a sustainable European tourism",
21 November 2003)

Tourism is already an important pillar for Europe. Annually, more than 400 million holidaymakers visit countries in the European Union. Together, they spend 300 billion. Thanks to the growth of the BRIC countries, the number of tourists visiting Europe in the coming 15 years will increase to 700 million.

Europe as one large open-air museum: that is the direction we are taking. Tourists will increasingly choose Europe, Europe will become the ideal holiday destination for tourists from around the world, particularly those from the new superpowers. France is currently the most popular worldwide holiday destination, and Spain in just behind the United States in fourth place. But the tourists who visit France and Spain are mainly from Europe itself: they are mainly the Dutch, Belgians, Germans and Brits. Tourism within Europe will increase further in the coming decades. Part-time living and a greying population are the causes of this. The large and growing group of seniors, upright in body and limbs, and living on pensions, will play a larger role in tourism within the continent. But in addition, a greater number of tourists can be expected from outside the continent, for example from Asia. In 2010, the European Union will discontinue the need for visas for Chinese

tourists. By 2020, India and China will have a middle class that is as large as the total European population. If Europe invests in "story-telling," and is capable of translating the magic of Paris, the beauty of Stockholm, the romance of Vienna and Sofia, the doll-like charm of Bruges and Amsterdam, the grandeur of Berlin, Madrid and Lisbon in stories that appeal to and attract Asian tourists, Europe can become one enormous Disneyworld.

Europe (in the form of national, regional and local authorities) will have to prepare itself for this. The question that has to be asked is: what will BRIC tourists want to see? They are known to prefer looking at sites that are clearly recognizable and interesting, such as original old buildings or copies of old buildings. In addition, they like spectacular new architecture, and want to visit areas where members of their own "tribe" live. The Chinese want to visit the Chinatowns in major cities and go out in clubs decorated in a Chinese manner, such as Jimmy Woo in Amsterdam or the China Club in the Adler Hotel in Berlin. Indians want to visit Little India (such as the London areas of Ealing, Brent, Harrow, Hounslow and Redbridge) Brazilians want to go to Little Rio, and Russians to Little Moscow. In these neighbourhoods they can network, do business, exchange knowledge and experiences, and shop. The bicultural population groups that live there play an important role in BRIC-tourism: they act as attractions.

In the field of architecture, the BRIC tourist wants something spectacular. It is significant that one skyscraper after another rises in Asia, each higher than the previous one. Malaysia has trumped Singapore in this skyscraper derby, and Taipei is ahead of Shanghai. India is not lagging behind, and even the skylines of Rio de Janeiro and Sao Paolo are becoming more and more impressive.

Boring and unexciting blocks of square boxes such as we build in our new estates do little for the BRIC tourist. Unfortunately, there is not much spectacular new architecture to be found in Europe, certainly not when compared with everything that is happening in

Asia, Sao Paolo and Dubai. We will have to develop more of this. The Guggenheim Museum in Bilbao is an example that should be followed, as should the Jewish Museum in Berlin and the Swiss Re building in London.

The retro-trend also offers possibilities. BRIC tourists also want authenticity, and BRIC tourism means a return to retro architecture in urban building. This is to the disgust of many urban planners and architects, who much prefer to make modern statements, but do not succeed very well in this. Square boxes can be easily decorated with retro-facades, decorative elements that can add a little spice to the depressing buildings, suggest the Dutch futurologists Das and Das. Municipal councils can demand that companies use retro lettering on their gables, something that is already happening in Rome: the Roman McDonald's has a gold M instead of the customary yellow one, and this fits in better with the city surroundings. This doesn't only make the BRIC tourist happier; in these times of insecurity, Europeans too have a longing for old familiar architecture.

Other retro products will also become popular for the same reason, for example "new old" cars, such as the Mini Cooper and the New Beetle. In Dresden, Germany, people decided to rebuild the old buildings after the allied bombing attack that destroyed the city during the Second World War. In Rotterdam (the Netherlands), a different choice was made, but there is now a great demand for "original" buildings. Discussions with Chinese show that they would like to have a second home in Rotterdam but would prefer to have an art deco apartment, many of which existed in Rotterdam prior to the war. If the needs of the BRIC tourist are taken into consideration, the Asianization of Europe will have an Old-European character.

Another branch that will attract tourists to Europe is wellness. BRIC tourists, and especially the rapidly increasing number of elderly in Europe, love it. This last group has time and money, and wish to spend their last years of life in relaxation. The ageing of the Netherlands and the rest of the European Union, China and Japan can be considered a drama but also an opportunity. Europe already has spas and health resorts, particularly in mountainous areas such as Switzerland, the Czech Republic and Austria. In Germany, the famous Heiligendamm health centre has been brought back to life, ready to welcome prosperous bon vivants from all parts of the world. Thermal baths, saunas, and a combination of yoga, sport and other relaxation techniques are a growth market. BRIC tourists, coming from hectic growth economies, will come to Europe for relaxation if Europe tackles this properly. In this context, the extensive areas of nature in Europe can also be exploited. Europe has many types of nature to offer: coast, wetlands, mountains, steppes, snow, forests and so on. The climate is so diverse that there is something for everybody, in all seasons. Putting Europe on the map because of its natural areas is not such a bad idea.

European interior design and architecture of tomorrow

Gonçalo Nuno Pyrrait Marques da Silva

Europe, design and architecture: they have been intertwined for centuries. In several European countries and regions, distinct architectural and interior styles have been created in the past. So architectural styles originate here which are typical for regions, as the *'vakwerkhause'* for Germany, the fortifications of Malta, the white houses of Greece and the wooden architecture of Scandinavia. All of these styles had their own distinctive interior designs and furniture, thriving in their own national or regional environments.

Globalization and migration changed things, naturally. In recent days German migrants in Brazil built *'vakwerkhause'* in the regions of Rio de Janeiro and Southern Brazil, Dutch migrants in the United States built replicas of Dutch traditional houses, and of course traditional Spanish and Portuguese architecture and interior design dominates South America. So European architecture and European architects were active in globalization, even in colonial times. Sometimes this led to fusion architecture, as in Indonesia where Dutch architecture mixed with local Indonesian styles, and new interesting mixed forms of architecture developed. All of this was reflected in the interiors. European interior designs, styles in furniture, lamps, carpets, curtains and other interior items found their way all over the world. The chandelier, for example, was created in Europe and found its way all over the world.

In the 21st century Europe will receive more tourists. They will visit our palaces, castles, mansions (some of them turned into museums, others into hotels) and other distinctive buildings, looking for the charm and romance of old Europe, yet enjoying modern comforts. Design will be one of the pillars of the future Europe. Interior design, traditionally one of Europe's unique selling points, will be an intrinsic part of the design industry of the future. Europe's design industry can only survive and thrive if it is different from design in the rest of the world. Quality of materials should be high, designs should be regionally distinctive, and there should be no room for low-quality products in the European interior of the future. *Stylish quality* should be our motto. Only then will the Asian and American tourists acknowledge us as 'special'.

If Europe wants to become an attractive tourist destination in the future, European designers should realize that more and more tourists from outside the continent want to see the real Europe. We should design accordingly. Yet there is room enough for new architectural styles and redevelopment of old buildings. For instance, in the German city of Leipzig *Die Baumwollspinnerei*, an old cotton factory, has been turned into the headquarters of a successful new art movement, the *Neue Leipziger Schule*. Artists live and work there, galleries and museums are booming, the old complex is modernized and has started a vibrant new life. In general the demolition of old buildings, just because they are too expensive to maintain, should be bound by strict rules. The fronts of old buildings should be kept in good condition, while behind them very modern and spectacular new buildings can be built. No cheap buildings: that happens too often in Europe. Let's change the face of Europe by building beautifully.

The Portuguese interior architect Gonçalo Nuno Pyrrait Marques da Silva works in several European countries. He specializes in the renovation, modernization and upgrading of mansions, palaces and other remarkable antique European buildings.

Pillar 2 *Knowledge economy*

One of the major causes for the stagnation of economic growth in Europe is the low level of investment in the knowledge economy. As we mentioned in the introduction, Europe no longer excels in anything, more and more students are leaving to attend better universities elsewhere, and inventions have their cradle in other parts of the world. The conclusion of the European Commission in Lisbon in 2000 and the OECD in 2001 was that the time has arrived for Europe (and other Western countries) to start investing once more in the knowledge economy. The Western economies need to be reshaped from factor-driven to innovation-driven. A strong knowledge economy offers possibilities for greater social prosperity, for a higher quality of life for as many people as possible, with respect for cultural values, for the natural environment (the environment and biodiversity), and for future generations. The most important aim of the Lisbon agenda is to create a dynamic and competitive knowledge economy. On the basis of this, the European Council held in Barcelona in March 2003 agreed that the average expenditure for

R&D and innovation should be at least 3 per cent of GDP. Two-thirds of this should be contributed by corporate life. In addition, a single large European Research Area (ERA) should be created, which will once again make Europe attractive for (top) researchers. At the same time a single European higher education area should be created, to promote student mobility. A single European research and higher education area will create a single European knowledge area.

At the moment, investments in R&D in Europe are not particularly inspiring. The way things are at the moment, we can divide Europe into three categories. First of all, there is a Premier League of a number of small countries – including Sweden and Finland – that annually invest more than 3 per cent in R&D. Next, there is a large group of second-division countries that invest something like the European average of 2 per cent in R&D. This division (R&D intensity between 1.5 and 2.5 per cent) is led by Germany (2.5 per cent) and Denmark (2.4 per cent); Slovenia (1.6 per cent) is the only recently admitted country that can claim a place in this division. The final division is made up of countries with R&D intensity below 1.5 per cent. The Czech Republic, Ireland and Italy head up this division. It includes, in addition to the majority of Southern member states, the newly admitted and candidate countries.

If the European Union wishes to achieve the 3 per cent across the board, then it is mainly the "old" members in the second division that will have to get their act together. It is important that they make sufficient progress. At the moment, attention is directed at the big four: Italy (with a worrying 1.1 per cent), the United Kingdom (with a not much better 1.8 per cent), France (2.2 per cent) and Germany (2.5 per cent). By creating the ERA, resources can be used more effectively. The ERA is concentrating on three problems: the fact that the research activities in Europe are fragmented and show overlaps, the fact that the environment for research and innovation is not particularly stimulating, and the fact that there is not enough financing for European research.

According to the European Commissioners, there are five matters that will be addressed by the ERA in the coming years. First, there will be financial project support for fundamental research based on international competition. Second, the European research capacity will be strengthened by removing obstacles for pan-European research and increasing transnational mobility. Extra support will be made available to young researchers. The third point is formed by pan-European private–public cooperation programmes, in the form of Technology Platforms categorized according to research areas. The fourth point is the promotion of European centres of excellence through networking and coopera-tion. And fifth, greater coordination must be created between national and regional research programmes (Source: SER – *More Growth with Europe*.)

There is, however, a but. Even if the 3 per cent norm is achieved, it will not automatically mean that the innovative capability of the European economy is strengthened. Spending more on innovation does not necessarily mean that you will get a better return. But it will be a start. It will put an end to the brain drain, because researchers will be able to do their research in Europe and not have to go elsewhere. These people are necessary to drive Europe forward: let us keep them here. We have already mentioned this movement: many people from Eastern Europe are returning from America to their home countries because, thanks to investments in the knowledge economy, there is now work for them there.

Pillar 3 *Service*

Europe is becoming less and less an industrial continent, and more and more a service continent. The seven OECD countries – the United States, Japan, France, Germany, the United Kingdom, Italy and the Netherlands – are the seven largest exporters of services; of these seven, five are in Europe. Germany, for example, earns more than 50 per cent of its GDP from services. Marketing, sales, administration, legal aid, consulting, but also cleaning services: that is what we do in Europe. Much of our industrial production is done in other countries – low-wage countries, to be precise. The Netherlands sells the most cocoa, even though it doesn't grow there. Large companies such as Philips, Nokia and Siemens have transferred large parts of their production to China and India, while marketing and sales are handled from their home countries. The European service sector is completely integrated into world trade and dependent on it. The EU is the

largest exporter of services in the world and the most important investor in services. The Union is responsible for 26 per cent of world exports in services (not counting exports within the European Union itself) compared with 24 per cent for the United States and 6 per cent for Japan.

The service sector could flourish even more if free transfer of services within the European Union could be fully leveraged. If the internal market were better integrated, the international competitive position of European corporations would be improved and their leading position in international trade strengthened. The conclusion of the European Council in Lisbon in 2000 was that for this to happen, a number of obstacles will have to be removed. Subsequently, the European Commission wrote an information paper entitled *An Internet Marketing Strategy for the Service Section* (29-12-2000). The most unambiguous sentence in this report was, "The service industry is the engine of the new economy." The Commission wrote further:

Technological change has made it absolutely essential that all unjustified obstacles for the free exchange of services should be removed. The competitive position of businesses increasingly depends on the most successful design and management of services and on a good integration of these in all management and sales activities. Many manufacturing companies now offer, in addition to products, services that create added value and differentiate them from their competitors. Efficient services have thus become an important engine of competition. Access to effective high-quality services is clearly of influence to the quality of life of the European citizen. Unjustifiable and avoidable obstacles that result in services being applied at a national rather than an internal market level is a matter that concerns us all.

According to the Commission, the tendency to think at a national level and only then to look at the larger market of the Union must be reversed.

That the obstacles have not yet been removed is illustrated by the fact that only a limited number of Europeans actually move around in Europe. The readiness among Europeans to move to another region or European country is minimal. In 2000 only 1.4 per cent moved to a different region, compared with 5.9 per cent of Americans, *Newsweek* reported. Even in the European Union, only 0.1 per cent of the total EU population – around 225,000 people – made use of their right to work and live elsewhere in the Union. Why is that? According to experts, there are various reasons. It could be that many Europeans are more attached to their home country than they admit, but there are clearer indications. According to the MEP Michael Cashman, one of the greatest barriers to a dynamic Europe is "the tendency for Member States not to recognize each other's qualifications". Anybody wishing to begin a hairdressing salon in Germany needs a German hairdressing diploma. Anybody who wishes to give ski lessons in France has to be in possession of a French ski diploma. These are forms of chauvinism that obstruct European unity and also, therefore, European dynamism. Europe is an enormous patchwork quilt of education standards, labour laws, medical care, social care and pensions. Every member state has its own rules. As long as such differences exist in the EU countries, a free trade of services will not be possible within the European Union.

With the "service directive", an expansion of the free trade of services and products found in the Treaty of Rome, Frits Bolkestein, in his function as European Commissioner for the Internal Market, wanted to make free trade of services easier and common practice. The directive received a lot of criticism, particularly from France. The French were afraid of "social dumping", which implies that, for example, Eastern Europeans would offer services at slashed prices in France and thus force their – relatively expensive – French competitors out of the market. Bolkestein thinks this argument is nonsensical:

> The directive adds nothing new to the existing treaties; it is simply a practical elaboration of them. The free trade of services was laid down in the original Treaty of Rome. And what are the French scared of? They are the fifth economy in the world and export a lot themselves. In addition, the free exchange of services will only be beneficial to the economy. We are especially talking here about small and medium-sized services; 70 per cent of small and medium-sized businesses are in the service industry. That can only grow further. And that economic growth is exactly what we need.

There are also critical voices. Heinrich Von Pierer, the former head of Siemens, believes that the service economy should not be idealized. Of course it is good for the service sector to expand, but it requires industry to make a service sector operate properly. He thinks Europe should retain its production industry come what may. Von Pierer has a point. You cannot expect Chinese and Indian tourists to buy things that are labelled "Made in Asia". They want things that are made in Europe. Thus there is, for them as well, a real market for "made here" manufacturing.

Pillar 4 *European industry*

This brings us to the fourth pillar: industry. There is still enough room for this. Despite sombre remarks to the contrary, Europe has a number of successes in this area. According to Jeremy Rifkin, whom we mentioned earlier, the French Airbus is larger than the American Boeing, and what's more, Europe has bigger construction and chemical industry sectors than the United States.

Airbus recently launched the A380, the largest passenger aircraft in the world, with a seating capacity for 800 passengers. It is the European answer to Boeing's 747 (the Jumbo). In the French daily *Le Figaro*, the headline above the A380 taking off was: "*Les ailes de l'Europe*" (the wings of Europe). The French determination to compete with America with a European aircraft industry has paid off.

A part of European manufacturing industry will, in the coming decades, be relocated to Eastern Europe. Various Western European companies have already done this, such as the German Opel. In the future, this will happen more frequently and more intensively. Eastern European countries are preparing themselves for this; it can put an end to their brain drain. Slovakia is a good example. In recent times, it has developed from a worrying regional infant to an economic tiger, partly because foreign car manufacturers relocated to the country.

The economic growth of Slovakia, however – and in 2004 it was 5.5 per cent – is highly dependent on the rest of the European Union. Approximately 85 per cent of all its exports go to EU member states. About three-quarters of all imports come from there, mainly from Germany and the Czech Republic. As a result of the general economic recession in the European Union, foreign investment dropped from US$4 billion in 2002 (an exceptional year) to just US$594 million in 2003.

At the moment there is once again a noticeable increase, largely influenced by the international car industry. The lion's share of GDP in Slovakia is realized by the service sector, followed by industry. After its partition from the Czech Republic in 1993, the country inherited a lot of heavy industry, particularly in the military sector. Agriculture is responsible for around 4 per cent of GDP. Wages in Slovakia are among the lowest in the European Union. The budget deficit is being tackled directly by the government in Bratislava. In 2003, it was nearly 5 per cent of GDP; a year later it was 3.8 per cent. In 2005 and 2006 the deficit has to drop below the European norm of 3 per cent. Thanks to important tax reforms, government income has increased.

Slovakia wishes to replace its kronen with the euro in 2009, and wishes to adopt the euro exchange mechanism (ERM2) in 2007. For this, inflation – in 2004 it was 7.5 per cent – must be lowered. Now the high unemployment level – according to the *Economist* Intelligence Unit, 14.3 per cent in 2004 – puts pressure on the budget. But it is decreasing: in March 2005 the lowest unemployment level since 1998 was achieved, at around 12 per cent.

Futures beyond the end of industrial history

Marco Bevolo

Here is a glimpse into the future of European design seen from the perspective of two global macro-trends and huge continental challenges.

The future of industrial design in Europe is a topic that firstly

Copyright Keiko Goto
(www.keikogoto.com)

generates several questions. These include, what is the future of both European industrial conglomerates and small to medium-sized enterprises? What is the future of the creative industry, both globally and continentally? What are the possible societal futures of this area of the planet, rich in material wealth but shaken in its existential foundations, as described by the likes of French novelist Michel Houllebecq? It is not the purpose of this short column to analyse the topic in depth. I would like to however point towards two global macro-trends that have been studied in recent years, and some pragmatic case histories which possibly anticipate how European design practices and communities might evolve.

Transformation

Europeans will increasingly look for those platforms and systems that enable them to evolve in their own lives, starting with newly defined communities of practice and shared interests. An integrated model of industry-design organization that might respond to this trend is the one of Italian districts. These regional concentrations of know-how developed in time as local clusters blessed by social harmony and high integration of very focused value chains, capable of reaching global success. The relevance of this approach to territorial and design integration is the focus of a newly launched Master's degree in Business Design at the Domus Academy of Milan, which aims to transfer to international students the "22design DNA" of the Italian model. Although it is being challenged by new global competitors, "Sistema Italia" might still offer elements for a new paradigm of industrial organization where design is a key success factor.

Diversity

On the other hand, the design of new cultural landscapes will be key for Europe. Either managed by means of inclusion or perceived as threat and tension, this will be the direction where the greatest achievements or the worst conflicts will continue to unfold in the next decade or more. Here the challenge to European design communities is to become evangelists of social integration, well beyond the line of duty of industrial styling. One of the best practices in this field – which one might want to call "cultural design"– is the work by Premsela, the Dutch foundation of design, which established an extensive programme of exhibitions and events to facilitate discussion about what "Dutch" design is, and how it can be developed to meet new challenges in society. The new "cultural frontiers" are the real opportunity for European creative leaders to make a deep impact on societies.

But the future of European design is deeply connected to the future of industrial Europe. What is the role of the creative industry in a declining mass-production economy? The destiny of some European brands might be foreseen in the acquisition of MG Rover by a former supplier from China. Successful European brands will become increasingly global with successful growth in emerging markets, which will result as well in a delocalization of competences like marketing and design towards Asia and other emerging areas. European design will then have to act as the integrator of design and cultures. Its role will be to connect people to people, both within companies and within markets. Facilitation will be the key, perhaps one day even over creation, in a truly inclusive process deploying the tools we know and use today, towards new futures.

Marco Bevolo is Design Director at Philips Design, a visiting lecturer at the Donau University of Krems, Austria and Domus Academy, and an advisory board member at Istituto Internazionale Studi sul Futurismo of Milan. He lives in Eindhoven, the Netherlands, and Turin, Italy.

Pillar 5 *Designer fashion and furniture*

Europe is traditionally good in fashion and design. In fact, Italy has changed the world more in this field than the United States. Fashion from Italy rules the world. Even in those countries that are gradually assuming a leading position in the world economy, such as China and India, Italian fashion is the favourite. Then there is Scandinavian design, largely in the fields of interiors (from IKEA to designer furniture), art (glass, sculpture), and architecture. German car designs determine the whole car industry worldwide.

The costs of manufacturing design articles are now fairly high in Europe. For this reason, goods with European designs (including fashion) will increasingly be produced in other countries. That is good for international sales. But tourists from China and India, who spend their holidays in Europe, will not want to buy fashion and design articles that were produced in their own countries. If they want to spend money here, it will be on exclusive articles. There is sufficient market for a European manufacturing industry, a fine economic pillar.

Take the Italian fashion industry. Thanks to a mix of craftsmanship and frivolity, the Italian fashion industry is the largest in the Western world, with a turnover of 66 billion in 2004. Per capita, the population of Italy earn more on fashion than Germany does on exporting cars, or Japan with its export of electronic equipment, says Mario Boselli, the president of the Italian fashion chamber. And yet there is a crisis, for Asia is a formidable competitor. "Made in Italy" looks as if it might lose out to "Made in China", since China gained access to the world clothing and textile market on 1 January 2005 thanks to the lifting of export quotas, and consumers throughout the world are eagerly purchasing cheap clothing from that country. H&M and Zara have based their success on this. China is already the largest clothing exporter, although it restricts itself to sportswear, underwear, socks and less complex clothing. The only way to alleviate the pressure from

China seems to be to offer high quality and to change collections more rapidly. If a collection changes quickly, the Chinese will not have time to copy the garments – after all, it takes 15 days for the boat from Hong Kong to reach Europe.

Faster changes in fashion is an answer, and so is entering into collaborations. The fashion industry in Italy is largely made up of old family companies, each of which individually lacks the strength to take on competition from China. A form of collaboration between the Italian fashion companies could change this. A third way of competing is for Italy to invest in China. Italy was rather late in doing this, and investments in China generally only start paying returns after ten years. In addition, the Italian fashion companies need to groom successors: important fashion designers such as Giorgio Armani, Luciano Benetton and Leonardo del Vecchio are all approaching 70 and have not yet named their successors. The question is whether sons, daughters, grandchildren, nephews and nieces are going to do the work, or whether it is better for the family members to take a step backwards and restrict their involvement to that of major shareholders, so that real managers can run the companies in the battle for the world market.

The same is true of the European furniture industry. It is rapidly losing ground to competitors from low-wage countries. In the European Union prior to expansion, the turnover of the furniture industry has shrunk by more than 8 per cent since 2000, to 8.1 billion, a reduction in turnover of more than 700 million. Employment dropped by almost 7 per cent to 927,000 jobs, according to figures from UEA (Union Européenne d'Ambeulement), the European Furniture Manufacturers Federation. Until 1999, the European Union exported more furniture than it imported; now, however, it imports more furniture than it exports – a deficit of 3.6 billion. In 1998, more than half the furniture produced worldwide came from the European Union; today that is 38 per cent.

Although the turnover of the furniture industry in the ten new EU countries is only worth 900 million, it has grown by 30 per cent in the last three years. Many Western European manufacturers have relocated their production to Eastern Europe, or are planning to do this.

Everything is aimed at competing with Asian manufacturers. The average wholesale price of a piece of furniture from China is 2 per kilo. For a piece of furniture from Middle or Eastern Europe, the price is 2.67 per kilo, and a Western European bed, sofa, cupboard or chest of drawers costs on average 4.54 per kilo. This is the major problem confronting the Western European furniture industry: its wholesale price is double that of its main competitors. In addition, there are EU import restrictions on components but not on complete furniture, and this stimulates a relocation of production to low-wage countries.

The European furniture manufacturers are currently working together to devise a solution. Although they do not seem to be in much of a hurry, it seems sensible for the European Union to protect its own furniture manufacturers in one way or another. But then the furniture industry will first have to report their problems to the European Union.

Pillar 6 *Food and wine*

Europe is traditionally famous for its culinary diversity. A lunch in Italy

is totally different from a dinner in Scandinavia, and this will become a marketing tool in the 21st century. Of course, busily occupied people want to eat quickly, and spending hours in the kitchen on a weekday will become increasingly rare. Nevertheless slow food is on the increase: particularly at the weekend, people spend a leisurely time at the table with friends and family enjoying quality home-made food. European wines are essential for local colour, even though we are drinking more wine from non-European countries, such as Chile, Argentina and South Africa.

European wines will remain important for tourists and for part-time residents. If you live for a few months each year in Bordeaux, then you are likely to prefer to drink local wine, and if you spend a couple of months in Tuscany, you will want to drink Tuscan wines. The same is true for the increasing group of tourists who come from places outside Europe. In export markets outside Europe, European wines will have greater difficulty in competing with products from the newly emerging wine countries.

What if ... this was the future of fruit?

Mike Port

"Fifth Conference of Producers of Products Equivalent to Fruit 2020" – the bold golden letters of the invitation catch my eye. I have to hurry in order to get to the location of the event, and flag down a taxi. I have been invited as guest speaker to enable delegates to learn what moves people to buy "traditional fruit" in spite of the high price. As a matter of fact, it has now become a rarity, so it is extremely expensive and mainly offered in gourmet restaurants and delicatessens.

The business of the "producers of products equivalent to fruit" is to change fruit, which is cultivated in giant monocultures, into these new-fangled fruit equivalents. For this purpose, the harvested fruit is pureed on the spot and made to go further, with tasteless substances, vitamins and nutrients added. Afterwards everything is pressed into a shape similar to the original fruit. At first sight, nobody would suspect that the skin of the fruit-equivalent banana was made of synthetic material and that of the fruit-equivalent apple of an edible natural fibre.

With this procedure the big combines have killed three birds with one stone. The processed fruit has a longer shelf-life, the fact that the exhausted land is hardly supplying any nutrients is compensated for by the added nutrients, and the new "skin" makes transport much safer. The main advantage, however, is that by adding the tasteless substances the harvested volume can be increased. In light of the exploding population this is a blessing. However, this is only one part of the offer. On the other hand, there are producers of the "traditional fruit" to which I belong. The power of the big boys has pushed us more and more into the background.

What they could not take away from us is our know-how when it comes to dealing with real fruit. As far back as the end of the 20th century, an important switch took place. Thanks to changing to organic growing we still have cultivable areas with extremely fertile soils. With us, treatment of the ripening fruit is still genuine manual work: the use of chemicals and mass-production processing techniques is completely out of the question. The result: extremely tasty fruit, without artificial additives, unlike the fruit equivalents.

Finally in the taxi I make up for missing a proper lunch. Although this is not very comfortable, it reflects the present trend. I have brought with me one of those new convenience meals, where opening the packaging produces a chemical reaction which, in a flash, heats the contents. As a result, nowadays people can enjoy hot meals anywhere they like. In order to reassure consumers, "made without genetically modified ingredients" is written on the multi-coloured foil of the lid, and I have to chuckle. By now, everybody knows that the last genetically modified plants were locked away three years ago, after it became obvious that it wasn't going to be possible to make them acceptable to consumers all over the world. Now, they are eking out a miserable existence in the safes of the research centres in case they are needed some day.

Only ten minutes to reach the congress centre, the taxi driver says. Plenty of time to take a quick glance at the newspaper. "According to a professor of biology, within five years' time the all-providing genetically engineered animal could become reality", the front page shows in bold letters, and I think: funny what the future will bring.

Mike Port (Germany) is director of Port International GmbH, international fruit traders since 1875. His company focuses on organic and fair trade markets and products.

Pillar 7
Environmental management and water management

The worldwide climate changes that are predicted for the beginning of the 21st century offer Europe economic opportunities. Eighty per cent of the world's population lives near water, and water management will therefore become an important issue in the 21st century. This covers a number of issues.

To start with, there is the use, distribution and recycling of drinking water, which is becoming scarcer. In this field, a lot of know-how has been accumulated in Europe. Spain is becoming drier and drier, and everything is being done to arrest the development of greater areas of desert, to improve irrigation, and to optimize the use of fresh water. North-West Europe has if anything surplus fresh water, and many European rivers have in the past few decades been diverted, or canals have been dug between them, partly in order to improve the distribution of drinking water and irrigation. This know-how can be exported to countries that need it: China, for example, where the area around Beijing is drying out, and India, where the same thing is happening around Delhi. European companies such as the Italian Piralesi have developed fresh-water recycling methods which are used on cruise ships, for example, and which can also be employed on land.

The gradual rise in sea level and in the level of water in rivers will also prove an important issue in the coming period. How can we manage this? How can we prevent flooding, and if it happens

213

nevertheless, how can we handle it best? Several European companies have thought up solutions to the problem. Houses that can be adjusted in height, anchored to a pillar, on the banks of rivers such as the Rhine and the Meuse; dykes, (flexible) dams, dredging work, sluices, and other ways of combating the rise in water levels – the ingenuity and creativity that can be brought to the problem can be seen throughout Europe. Venice is being protected against flooding with flex-dams which are now being constructed in the sea. In other cities too, such as those that lie on rivers that already flood their banks (Dresden, Prague) a whole variety of measures have been developed to handle this. This know-how can also be exported.

Another issue is environmental management. First get rich, if necessary with pollution as a consequence, and then, when you're rich enough, clean up the pollution and the environment. That has been Europe's policy over the past 60 years. That will also be the policy of the new polluters, such as the Asians. So be it. By the time they get round to cleaning up the environment, they can make use of the know-how built up by the Europeans – for a small fee. And Asians who do not want to live (permanently) in a polluted continent can always lodge – full-time or part-time – in Europe. The empty houses will thus be put to good use.

Pillar 8 *Care and wellness*

A lot will be earned in the coming decades on care, care tourism and wellness – in short in the well-being of people. This branch will grow enormously, for example because of ageing. Many elderly Europeans will invest more in their body condition and health, so that they will be in shape to live as long as possible. Quality of life will become important, and we will be prepared to pay for it – from cosmetics to plastic surgery, from sport to meditation, from massage to acupuncture, from mental gymnastics to voluntary work: everything for a healthy mind in a healthy body.

Conclusion

The aims of Lisbon 2000 were wonderful; by 2005, little had actually taken place. This can be attributed to a variety of factors. The collapse of the Internet market, failing economies and, as a result of this, hesitant citizens who do not dare to take risks are some of these. In addition there are several European countries, including France and Germany, that do not wish to conform to the reforms prescribed by "Europe". That is why the President of the European Commission Jose Manuel Barosso introduced new aims at the beginning of 2005, which are more modest. In a nutshell, he suggests that the member states should set themselves three priorities: creating more jobs, technological renewal and creating a better climate for investors in their countries. Barosso believes that this would help create 6 million new jobs by 2010 and allow the economy to grow by 3 per cent. At the moment, the growth is 2 per cent.

The Commission also considers it important to resolve the problem of youth unemployment in Europe. Young people are necessary to contribute to the costs of ageing, but there are not so many young people, and many of them are unemployed. Between 2005 and 2050, the number of young people between the ages of 15 and 24 will drop by a quarter, from 12.6 per cent of the population to 9.7 per cent, while the group of 65-plussers will grow from 16.4 per cent to 29.9 per cent. Youth unemployment at the moment stands at 17.9 per cent, compared with 7.7 per cent among people older than 25. Young people have a greater chance of falling into poverty – 19 per cent of those aged between 16 and 24, compared with 12 per cent of those between 25 and 64.

Young people are essential, however, if the aims of Lisbon are to be achieved, since they form the future labour market and what's more are the future source for research capacity, innovation and entrepreneurship. The Lisbon aims can only be achieved if young people are adequately equipped with knowledge, skills and competencies through good and relevant education and training. In order to achieve that, poverty and social exclusion must be combated, as must also

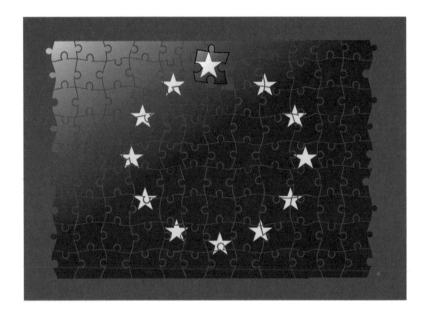

discrimination against women in the labour market. The European Commission wants to move forward towards a European valuation system for diplomas and the like, to ensure that young people are encouraged to learn more foreign languages, and that skills for independent entrepreneurship are given more attention in education.

How all this will work out remains to be seen. The alarm bells are ringing insistently – as shown by the remarks by Ben Bot quoted at the beginning of this chapter. If nothing happens, we can write off Europe. Then we will move towards the Argentinean model. If Europe actually invests in the pillars mentioned here and removes the obstacles to such pillars, however, we can achieve much in the 21st century.

Megatrend **7**

Towards European cultural renewal

Introduction

European cultures are singular, unique and old. They have always been changing. Since the end of the Second World War they have been peaceful. Never before in history has peace existed for such a long stretch of time in this old continent, which is due to the successful model of the European Union and the intermingling of European economies. Europeanization first created 25 to 30 countries out of more than 2000 regions in Europe in order to create larger internal markets when modern capitalism emerged, and now it is creating one Europe out of these countries, when globalization makes still larger markets necessary. More and more young Europeans tend to feel European first, then identify with their nationality. Slowly a new European identity is emerging out of the several national identities we used to have.

In times of globalization and Europeanization a strong identity is needed, and Europeans tend to seek and find their new strong identity in their region or city. So Europeanization is strengthened by regionalization and cityfication. Europeans will be inspired to develop a new hybrid identity that on one hand embraces a

European identity, and on the other hand values the local culture of the place they are rooted in. The new Europe in this sense will be more or less a conglomerate of 2000 or more city-states, making the nation-state less important, as was stated before.

As I argued before that in times of globalization, regionalisms and nationalisms are needed to give people strength, so I argue that in times of tremendous scientific achievements, religion and spirituality are needed, in order to cope with the technological revolution. The Cardinal of Bologna, Giacomo Biffi, said in the year 2000, "I believe that Europe will become either Christian or Islamic in this new century." The observation of the Cardinal might be proven right sooner than many would have thought.

I argued in the introduction of this book that spirituality in several forms is getting back into the mainstream of European societies, despite the fact that Europe was until recently one of the least religious continents on earth. For example, in the draft of the European Constitution, no God is mentioned, which is different from the United States and many other countries or regions. The Constitution is purely concerned with business. Yet spirituality and religion are emerging once again as major pillars of the identity of the European people of the 21st century.

Several forms of rechristianization have been seen, especially of central and eastern European regions. Rechristianization is also taking place in several regions in Scandinavia and Western Europe. Sometimes traditional Christianity is being practised again, but often people don't go to church, but communicate more intensively with priests, evangelical Catholic and Protestant churches. Such movements are operating in more European regions now than ten years ago. Younger generations have their own ways of expressing and designing their religious lives: "God is like XTC" was to be read at a Christian event for young Europeans lately. Religion is also coming back into politics, as was to be seen in Poland where in 2005 a religious president was elected.

This rechristianization is also an answer to Islam, which is on the rise in Western Europe. There a certain style of Islamization is seen due to the large numbers of Islamic immigrants who have been settling there in the past 50 years, and of course the international megatrend of the tension between Christianity and Islam is felt more strongly in areas where believers in the two religions live together than in areas where people of only one of these two denominations live. So Cardinal Biffi is gradually proven to be right, only in a different way than he might have thought: Central and Eastern Europe, and finally also Scandinavia, might become Christian again, and

Western and major parts of Southern Europe might become Islamic (Britain, France, the Netherlands, Belgium, Spain, some parts of Italy and Portugal, and some parts of Germany) and merge with Northern Africa and probably Turkey to form Eurabia. So it is my expectation that Europe in the 21st century will finally be split up into a Christian part and an Islamic part.

I do not expect that the border between the two parts will be as heavily secured as East and West Europe were divided during the era of the Cold War. The border will be more diffuse, because both Europes will trade with each other. After all, free trade is in the interests of both. I expect that Islamic enclaves will exist within some Christian parts of Europe, and in certain Islamic parts of Europe Christian enclaves will exist, although the option is not to be ruled out of the future leaders of the two new blocs deciding to exchange tribes of people, as the leaders of Turkey and Greece did at the beginning of the 20th century. Then all the Greeks in Turkey moved out and resettled in Greece, and all the Turks in Greece moved out and resettled in Turkey, in this way reducing the tensions in the several mixed areas where these two groups of people had lived before. This kind of 'peoples exchange' might occur again.

Another option might be more practical: every bloc accepts religious minorities within its borders, but demands higher taxes from them than from the rest of the population. This was the way the Moorish and Ottoman Islamic empires treated and protected the Jewish and Christian minorities within their borders for centuries. This old way of living apart while together might be revived in the new Europe.

Within Europe a new power shift is taking place at the beginning of the 21st century. New energy is emerging in Eastern Europe, where a new generation of well-educated and ambitious young politicians and entrepreneurs is taking power and modernizing their countries and regions. The United States is their source of inspiration, and not Western Europe. More Western European companies are investing in the East, more work is outsourced from West to East, more

Easterners work in the West. Within Germany, which is part of East and West, since 2005 two East Germans have been the two most influential political leaders, something that would have been unthinkable before. This process is called the easternization of Europe. In the near future this will rapidly increase.

The European regions have to deal one way or another with the new economic world order, as described in the first chapter of this book: an order in which the major economic power shifts towards Asia, especially to China and India. This process of the Asianization of the world will also materialize in Europe. We shall welcome more Asian tourists in the future. We shall trade more with Asia, and we shall gradually learn to accept the new Asian domination of the world.

All of these trends will together merge in the megatrend of the European cultural renewal.

Asianization

We have said it earlier: during the 21st century, four new economic superpowers will join America and Japan – Brazil, Russia, India and China, known collectively as the BRIC countries. Very soon, three and a half of the six superpowers will be located in Asia (Russia is half European), and their new position of power will result in an increasing Asianization in many countries. The rise of Japan as an economic superpower in recent decades only resulted in a very limited Japanization of Europe, even though many Europeans have the image of hordes of Japanese tourists burned on their inner eye. But electronics and automobile brands and Japanese restaurants have not been enough to change the look of European streets.

The emerging moguls from Asia are of a different nature from Europeans and also from the Japanese. They are self-assured and self-aware. India rejected all European offers of aid following the tsunami of Christmas 2004. The country is working on its rebuilding under its own power, and even provided help as regional superpower to other affected countries, such as Sri Lanka and Indonesia. India is now claiming a permanent seat on the Security Council of the United Nations. The China–India axis that was recently forged in a collaboration treaty has big ambitions. This must be their century, the century of Asia. In part that is revenge for the past, in which Europe dominated Asia. India was governed by Europeans for a long time, and China too was under European influence (during the period of a weakened emperor and the period of the communist takeover in 1949, when the country was plunged into unrest and internal (opium) wars raged). The political leadership of neither country has forgotten this, and in the 21st century they plan to take revenge on Europe. They are aware that they now hold the trumps, and they want to make use of them before their luck changes.

But there are more reasons. China was a superpower earlier in its history. At the time of the Han dynasty (from the second century BC to the second century AD), the Tang dynasty (from the sixth to ninth centuries), and the early days of the Ming dynasty (the 14th to 15th centuries), China was a superpower, with greater influence than even the Roman Empire in its heyday. That whets the appetite for more. China has always viewed itself as the centre of the world: the Chinese called their country the "Empire of the Middle". The first Emperor Xin gave the united empire this title in the third century BC, with complete justification.

Every tribe within the human race has a superiority complex to a certain degree; these Asian tribes have it as well. China goes so far as to withhold Chinese citizenship from immigrants who are not ethnically (totally) Chinese. They can obtain a resident's permit, but nothing more. That was the fate of North Vietnamese and

Korean brides who entered China to marry Chinese men (the surplus of men as a result of the Chinese policy of one family, one child makes this necessary). It was also the fate of non-Chinese inhabitants of Hong Kong, when the territory reverted to China after a century of being a British crown colony. This arrogance and self-assurance will be expressed by Asians in Europe as well.

Tourists

Many visitors from Asia will shortly come to Europe to gape in amazement. They will come in large numbers and bring their culture with them. They are, as we said, more self-assured than the Japanese, and will become more dominant in the street scene and culture of Europe. We are speaking here particularly of Chinese and Indians. The World Tourism Organization expects that the numbers of visitors to Europe from China and India will increase considerably in the coming decades. In 2003 China surpassed Japan for the number of people visiting foreign destinations; in total, around 20.2 million Chinese made trips abroad. China will soon have a middle class that is as large as the total European population – 300–400 million people. The same applies to India. People from this class in particular enjoy travelling to Europe, which they regard as one large Disneyland, an enormous "human zoo".

Thus, Europe in the 21st century will undergo a double change of ethnicity. The population will become more multi-ethnic, but so too will the tourists. Thanks to the increase in the number of Chinese and Indians in the streets of European cities, the street scene will become more Asian, and we shall soon hear more Mandarin and Hindi than English in the vicinity of the major attractions. This will make it easier to become accustomed to Asians as the new moguls of the world. They won't remain at a distance; they will come to visit our continent, which will change into one enormous open-air museum for tourists from all corners of the world.

That Chinese and Indians are expected to visit Europe in large numbers is a great opportunity. Worldwide tourism is growing and becoming a main economic pillar. Besides, American tourism to EU countries decreased in the last years. This trend is expected to be continued in the future. They will concentrate on tourist areas in their own country or in South America. This is already noticeable in countries such as Argentina and Brazil. Domestic tourism in the US will also increase considerably.

India on the North Sea, Europe in Mumbai

Liesbeth van Dijk

There's a lot of good happening in the field of Indian– European entrepreneurship. Philips has announced how successful it is in India and the European media immediately latch on to this. Yet the Asian focus of the media is more generally directed at China. Various European entrepreneurs are successful in India; various Indian entrepreneurs are successful in Europe, traditionally primarily in the UK, but increasingly throughout continental Europe. This happens in a variety of different fields.

The outsourcing of various activities by European companies to India is increasing. There will be more tourism in Europe from India, and there is a market in India for European creativity and inventiveness in a wide range of areas, from water management and design to exceptional restaurant and bar concepts. Europe is assuming a place on the map of India; European banks, led by ABN Amro, are seeing these opportunities and are becoming increasingly active in India. For ABN Amro, India is one of the most important countries in which it is active. A lot of significant work is being done by the Dutch–Indian Chamber of Commerce and similar organisations in other European countries.

A lot is also happening at the level of individual entrepreneurs. That should be communicated better. There are still too few European stakeholders who see the business growth potential in India. Still too few European entrepreneurs from various branches make use of the possibilities in India. People are unaware of them, India still has the wrong image for them, and unknown is unloved. In addition, people are apprehensive about culture divides and different ways of doing business.

Vak Zuid has been active in India for two years, and with success. The restaurant/bar annex network concept of Vak Zuid that is so successful in Amsterdam has been introduced successfully in Mumbai, and plans are now underway to expand it to other Indian cities. With this concept we want on the one hand to create more interest and support in Europe for doing business in India, and on the other to make Indian stakeholders more aware of the possibilities of doing business in Europe, particularly on the European continent.

As the leaders of this initiative, we want to stimulate, promote and encourage entrepreneurship. Relying on the government is not enough. If we want to stimulate entrepreneurship, it is vital that we keep a list of learning experiences, bottlenecks, tips and advice concerning European–Indian business activities, and make this available to a wide circle. In this way, they can act as an example, as "storm troopers" for this new business venture.

Various factors for success in European-Indian business have, it is true, been assessed in scientific and other publications, research reports and policy papers. But they have not yet been translated into accessible practical information for business people. The personal accounts of European entrepreneurs in India, and vice versa, are often only known to a small circle. The personal stories of these entrepreneurs provide a good source of inspiration for business people aspiring to enter this market, and must therefore be communicated to wider circles. For Europe and India can, in this new Golden Age, do a lot of good for each other. Churchill once expressed a truth that is just as applicable today: "This is no time for ease and comfort. It is the time to dare and endure."

Liesbeth van Dijk mediates on European–Indian entrepreneurship.

Business people

In addition to Chinese tourists, we shall also receive a growing number of Chinese business people. In 2001 China joined the World Trade Organization, which considerably simplified trade with it. In 2005 the European Union is the largest non-Asian trading partner of China after the United States, in both imports and exports. It is true, however, that the European Union imports more from China than it exports there – in 2003 the difference was US$55 billion – because China is not an easy market to penetrate. Anybody wishing to sell products in China needs persistence and patience in order to break through the bureaucracy, discriminatory regulations and price controls.

For the time being, the story will largely be about imports from China. China will soon become the world's factory: one in five products will be manufactured there. This will be preceded by a stormy development. We can talk about the "Wild East" in this context. My friend Hans Lensvelt, CEO of Lensvelt BV in Shanghai, told me an interesting anecdote.

Here in Shanghai I recently made the acquaintance of Mr Dali Sun. I think he is worth around US$2 million. We make use of steel with a thickness of 0.9 mm – not a particularly common thickness, so it can't be bought everywhere, but Dali Sun has it. All at once we couldn't buy it anywhere, except from Dali Sun. Last week he paid me a visit: "Hans, I've bought up all the stocks in the city of 0.9 mm steel for US$20 million." That's nice for him, I thought. "How are you going to pay for it?" I asked. Answer: "You're going to pay for it, because you're my friend." "I beg your pardon?" "You can buy it from me for just 20 per cent more." And so Dali Sun earned 20 per cent of US$20 million. That's how things are in the 21st-century "Wild East". People take enormous risks; ambition and forward thinking ooze out of many Asians; they do not allow themselves to be distracted by tsunamis, pollution and traffic jams. Entrepreneurial behaviour and risk-taking are preferable to risk-avoidance, which seems to be the norm in Europe.

Style

If Europe wishes to welcome its Asian visitors in style, we shall have to adapt ourselves to Asian tastes and opinions, norms and values. Europeans will have to realize that many Asians simply do not understand European differences that are cherished here. Just as many Europeans have difficulty in distinguishing between Chinese ("they all look alike"), so many Chinese find it difficult to distinguish one white from another ("they all look alike"). When I came to live in Europe in 1983, I found it difficult to distinguish between all those white Europeans. It took me years to see the difference. Europeans will therefore have to invest in making themselves recognizable and distinguishable.

New building estates in Amsterdam look the same as those in

Milan and Frankfurt. Why would a Chinese tourist want to be photographed in front of one of these anonymous towers, which are interchangeable with each other? Why would an inhabitant of Shanghai or Hong Kong, which boast some of the most spectacular new architecture (much of it designed by European architects, such as Rem Koolhaas who designed the new building for Chinese State Television in Beijing) pay out good money to view anonymous, indifferent new architecture here? There is little new architecture in Europe that would appeal to this group. The Guggenheim museum in the Spanish city of Bilbao, the Jewish Museum in Berlin, the Swiss Re building (the "gherkin") in London – those will appeal. Those would make you sit up even in Asia. But otherwise? Asian tourists want to see typical European architecture or good replicas of that. They aren't fussy. But they don't like the soul-less architecture that has ruined much of the European landscape. They've got that at home, too. Don't forget: most Asian cities are ugly and will just get uglier.

Alex Kerr rightly criticizes the ugliness of modern Japan. Modern China, India and the Asian tigers are just as ugly. There are beautiful spots in Asian cities (the Royal Palace in Bangkok, the Red Fort in Delhi, the Bund in Shanghai, the 101 building in

Taipei, the Petronas Tower in Kuala Lumpur, the new city of Putrajaya in Malaysia), but on the whole they are terribly ugly. China now has plans to build new cities for 400 million people in the coming years (urbanization is increasing so rapidly that the existing cities cannot handle the arrival of newcomers from the country areas) which will probably be just as ugly and anonymous and indifferent as so much modern Chinese building. If people see so much ugliness at home, they will want to see picturesque, authentic, typically European architecture on their holidays to Europe. A revival of retro-building in Europe – as British Prince Charles has so often and repeatedly advocated – is entirely appropriate. But

demolishing all the new buildings that have been put up during the last 60 years is also a form of capital destruction. One option is to stick new retro facades on the boils on the face of European cities, or spectacularly modern faces. It is all about scenery: only the form makes the content matter, don't you think?

Clothing

Something similar is true of clothing. Don't expect an Indian or Chinese tourist to buy a souvenir or a dress made in Asia. That's not what they come for. People want things made here, so there is a large enough market for European manufacturers aimed at serving these large groups of new consumers visiting Europe. People don't want to buy things here that are also available in shops back home. What's the point of buying a dress from H&M in Copenhagen which is also in the shops in Tokyo, Mumbai or Beijing? Tourists can't really go home with something like that. European products, European design, in limited series, made to suit their taste (in colours, fabrics and so on) will have a good future.

Many Asians are smaller than Europeans. They have different clothing sizes. I once saw in Oslo how a Chinese tourist was directed to the children's department (the Scandinavians and the Dutch are the tallest Europeans, even the tallest people in the world). He was not amused. We shall therefore soon see adult clothing in European boutiques in a wide range of sizes for both

European and Asian customers. (There are, of course, tall Asians, for example in the Indian state of Rajasthan.) But in the range of consumer products, European manufacturers and retailers will have to realize that Asians have different tastes, and that this is culturally determined. White is the colour of death in China, for example, and designers will need to take this into account. Many middle-class people in Asia have smaller homes than those in Europe, so they can't fill up their apartments with lots of trinkets. People typically buy relatively cheap articles with a short life (a T-shirt they wear for a few months and then throw away) or relatively expensive articles with a long life (a fur coat that will last for generations, or jewellery or an expensive watch). Nothing middle of the road: middle of the road is a dead-end road.

Food

"Out of the box" thinking is also required for food. In Europe, we eat traditional food from the ground: meat, pasta, potatoes, vegetables (cabbage, carrots, leeks). In Japan, people eat a lot of food based on water: rice, fish, seaweed. There are people who claim that Japanese women suffer less from breast cancer than European women because of the food they eat. Perhaps that is true. In China and India people also eat a lot of rice, and this is increasingly genetically modified. In Europe, the lobby against GMOs is still very strong, but it will ultimately lose the fight, if only because the Asians think the discussion senseless. The world population will grow from 6 billion to 9 billion by 2050, and without GM food, famine will be widespread. Whole tracts of uncultivated land would have to be sacrificed for agricultural purposes, and that is really not necessary.

The mass arrival of Asian tourists will mean that more Asian food (either fusion or traditional) will be eaten in Europe. Noodle restaurants are shooting up like mushrooms in many European cities, and traditional European food manufacturers now supply supermarkets with Asian or Asian-inspired ready-to-eat meals or meals in a packet. European menus will include more and more Asian dishes or fusion food. Of course Asians will want to try something from the European kitchen, but they do not really like European food. That's OK, and Europeans are beginning to enjoy Asian food more and more, as is shown by the success of Asian and fusion restaurants in a whole variety of cities, all targeted at the European clientele.

A manager of the Indian multinational Tata who lives in the Uruguayan capital Montevideo recently sighed to me: "I do so miss Indian spices, but there are only 20 Indians here, the market is far too small, and so we have to make do with this cowardly Spanish-type food they serve here. Bah!" Anyway, when Indians wander through European cities in groups of ten, there will be a large enough market for their eating habits. Restaurants will also start serving Asian-style vegetarian food (that is, vegan food that does not contain any dairy products), and as well as people eating food with Western cutlery, it will become normal and widespread for them to use chopsticks or (in traditional Indian fashion) to eat with the right hand. Although, of course, there is cultural crossover working in the opposite direction: Chinese in the cities now eat with Western cutlery.

There are also attempts in Asia to cook in the European style, but not always with success. I recently ate with my partner in a top restaurant in India. I chose Indian food and it was perfect. He, a lover of all things Italian, wanted to try the pasta. It was disgusting. When the cook came to ask respectfully whether the food had been to our liking, my partner told him how awful it had been. The chef was furious and totally unaware of having done anything wrong. The pasta had been perfect by his standards. Italian and Indian kitchens are light years apart from each other.

Decadence

Most Asians from the higher classes are not so very sober. In Jakarta I saw how several ladies of the local elite had themselves taken round the city in their chauffeur-driven limo. It was 35° outside, but the air conditioning in the limo ensured that inside the conditions were arctic, so that the ladies could wear their chinchillas and sip champagne while they discussed the way things were in the world. Asian decadence? Wonderful!

The price of fur rose in 2003 by 20 per cent, simply because of the increasing demand from China. One question that is raised is, how shall we deal with environmental terrorists in the future? A scene in 2020: a Chinese grande dame is strolling through the streets of Amsterdam wearing a fur coat, doing her Christmas shopping, and making the local shop owners extremely happy. Suddenly an environmental terrorist throws a can of paint over her fur coat. What happens then? Can this go as unpunished then as it does now? And how will the environmental terrorists deal with the fact that fur has become fashionable throughout Europe? It has always been perfectly acceptable in Russia, Eastern Europe, Germany, Spain and Scandinavia; and Denmark and the Netherlands are the largest exporters of fur in the world. Virtually all fashion designers, with their eye on the new luxury market, are using fur again, now frequently shaven and dyed (often candy pink or vivid green), and aimed at the younger market. Fur is once again part of the street scene. The animals that give their lives for these coats are killed in the same way as the cows for our steaks – with an electric shock, so the idea of animal cruelty that hangs around is no longer relevant. That doesn't seem to have penetrated the minds of the anti-fur brigade.

Service

The Asian love of Italian haute couture causes problems. Chinese tourists buy so much in Italian shops that there is nothing left for Italian customers. This results in racist incidents and shouting matches. Add to this the fact that Chinese consumers are accustomed to a different type of service in shops. They consider the nine-to-five mentality that characterizes most of Europe's shops ridiculous. Chinese assume that if they enter a shop just before closing time, it will stay open until they have finished their business, as usually happens in Asia. That is not (yet) the case here, certainly not in countries and branches where the old trade unions still have all the power in their hands (some parts of Germany) or where old values are still dominant. During a recent visit to Bordeaux I wanted to go into an antiques shop, the closing time of which was unknown to me, only to have the door slammed shut in my face with the explanation that the owner was going off to eat. Eating is sacred for the old French, and they are even prepared to sacrifice possible extra turnover to it.

But such an attitude is unthinkable for a shopkeeper in Asian cultures. Trade before food is the rule there. The Spanish siesta is also unthinkable for Asians. The Spanish government wants to reduce the siesta, however, and is currently working hard on this. Various shops now stay open in Spain during the afternoon.

Europe and the new *feng shui*

Gita Kapoor

The Asianization of Europe in the 21st century will happen in several ways at the same time. One thing is for sure: more Asians will buy or rent European real estate in the near future. And more Asians will visit Europe, which is becoming a more and more interesting holiday destination for the growing Asian middle and upper classes. Not only Chinese, but also Indian and other Asian

233

investors regard property in not only commercial but other terms. They inspect the horoscope of a building. Will it bring them good luck or not? The horoscope of a building is called *feng shui*. It will become more relevant than ever in the new Europe.

Feng shui, originating in China more than 5,000 years ago, has in the last part of the 20th century become a part of architecture, building development, and home living, in both Asia and the West. Yet in Asia more people are applying it in their homes or office than in Europe. But *feng shui* is not just something for the Asian mind: its overall application is fundamental to all people's well-being. As Europeans will have more say over their space in the future, with more of them working from their homes (services are more important in the new Europe than industrial work), we will see the use of *feng shui* become more prevalent. Some European interior designers are already using *feng shui* with their clients, and the next untapped profession that will start using *feng shui* in Europe will be real estate agents. Real estate is ideal for this, especially for "hard to sell" properties, and there are quite a lot of them in Europe.

Feng shui is developing more into a mathematical science nowadays. Traditional *feng shui* is based on four aspects: building, environment, people and time. Just as the earth is constantly moving and changing, so are the energies of *feng shui*. Modern science has shown that geomagnetics are in a state of constant flux. *Feng shui* calculations show changing results based on the variables of building, people, time and environment. In the 21st century a new *feng shui* is developing. It mixes traditional *feng shui* with modern science, globalization and the new energy circuits that are developing in the new economic world orders, as is described in this book. In a sleeping country there are other energy circuits then in a tiger country, for example. *Feng shui* is developing into a lifestyle, a system of analyzing people's energy.

Feng shui's methodologies will be more like Western scientific inquiry in the 21st century. *Feng shui* practitioners will observe and record, formulate mathematical models of structures, and report findings in both technical and lay people's language. As more Asians live part-time or full-time in Europe, more Asians visit Europe during holiday or business trips, Asian-European trade and business relations intensify, you will see more about *feng shui* being written in European magazines, newspapers, and more exposure will be given to it on television and radio. As *feng shui* awareness grows in Europe, property investors will realize that it's easier to sell a building that is built according to *feng shui,* because the market is larger this way: they include potential Asian buyers in their range, new and necessary in an age of globalization.

Gita Kapoor is based in the Indian capital of Delhi. She is a feng shui master and works for the World Bank, Citibank, Intercontinental Hotels and several other major international companies. Her columns and articles appear in leading Indian newspapers like the Times of India *and the* Hindustan Times.

Bicultural style

It helps if Asians see other Asian faces in European shops, companies and products. Then they will have at least one recognizable point of reference. It helps that so many Chinese already live and work in Europe: these bicultural, multilingual Europeans can provide a useful bridge with Chinese tourists. In the future, we can expect more Chinese and Indian films in Europe on television and in the cinema (and the integration of television and Internet will make even greater diversity possible), and European–Asian co-productions in the field of film, theatre, musicals and so on will become increasingly common. In European schools, more children will learn Chinese and Hindi, as is happening now in Asia. Chinese is now taught in many schools and universities in Asia. In Japan, Chinese is now the third language in universities, after Japanese and English. Although some

2 billion of the 6 billion people on earth speak English, and English will remain the language of business, Mandarin Chinese is expected to develop into an additional trading language. It is therefore worth investing in this, even if it is only because you can only learn to know a people if you speak their language. Language says much about culture, about the way people think.

In other areas, too, Europe is interesting for Asians. India's Bollywood annually produces more films than America's Hollywood (excluding, by the way, the American porn industry). Many films include scenes on snow-covered mountains. These used to be filmed in Kashmir, but because of the unrest there they are now filmed in Europe, mainly in Switzerland. That has an additional advantage. Because the location is so far away from India, the stars are not constantly absent from the set to attend day-long wedding celebrations or other parties organized by family members. And let's be honest: a mountain is a mountain, and who sees the difference between the snow-covered peaks in the Alps and the snow-covered peaks in the Himalayas?

Chinatowns

The Chinese diaspora is spread throughout the world, and in Europe the Chinese are well represented. Migration from China to Europe is still high. More and more Chinese immigrants are settling in Southern and Eastern Europe, with Hungary the remarkable leader, with more than 10,000 Chinese. Italy and Spain are also popular countries for Chinese immigrants. What is remarkable is that the Chinese now come from a variety of regions. They used to come primarily from the provinces of Zhejiang and Fujian, but with the closing of the mines and factories in the Northeastern provinces, more Chinese immigrants are coming from there.

The Chinese prefer to live together, in common with many immigrants. Many of the Chinese who have come to Europe live in the Chinatowns that have arisen in many European cities: Madrid, Berlin, The Hague, Naples. These Chinatowns attract large numbers of Chinese tourists who like to see how their countrypeople live here.

This is a good reason for investing in these Chinatowns and transforming them into a means of promoting European–Chinese trade.

In Europe there are a large number of people of either fully or partly Indian origin, the majority in the UK. On the European mainland, the majority – around 300,000 – live in the Netherlands, mainly in the area around The Hague. It is, in fact, the Delhi of the European continent. The same is true here as for the Chinatowns: we should use them for bicultural trade relations. Those who have colonial and trade experience in Asia know how Asians think, feel, consume and travel, and know their norms and values. What's more, Asians can relate more easily to those with this experience, if only because there are buildings and other remains of the colonial past in their countries.

The French can profit from their Indo-Chinese past (Vietnam, for example, has many buildings of French origin), the Dutch from their past in Indonesia (they governed there for 300 years and the national language Bahasa-Indonesian has absorbed many Dutch words), the British from their past in India, and the

Spanish from their past in the Philippines. European countries with experience in Asia have a headstart on other European countries, and can turn this lead to their advantage.

Beauty

Power is erotic. Henry Kissinger, former US Secretary of State for Foreign Affairs, once said: "Power turns even the ugliest frog into a fairy-tale prince, and I am the best example of that." The good man was indeed as ugly as hell, but always scored with the most beautiful women. In the new century, this will happen on a large scale. At the moment most Europeans do not consider most Asians sexy, but that is starting to change.

The ideals of beauty are always determined by style icons, and style icons generally come from rich, powerful areas. Part of their attraction is because they are not only beautiful but also are icons of power. Jackie Kennedy was a symbol of beauty, but also of a powerful America. The same is true of Madonna. David Beckham is a symbol of beauty, metro-sexuality, physicality, the West, and the new rich. Very soon we shall have new style icons from the East. They can also be ethnically ambiguous, such as J-Lo.

The ideals of beauty will undergo a re-evaluation in Europe. Skin, for example, will be kept as pale as possible (perhaps using whitening, skin creams, which are eagerly purchased by Asians). New make-up lines already simulate a paler face instead of the toasted brown that was the fashion for so long. Already, make-up is used to make the eyes appear slanted. Already hair fashions from the East (long and straight, with fewer perms) are popular in Europe. More Asian influences will also be seen in clothing. Exposed bellies (they originated in India and it doesn't matter if you have love-handles) are also seen in Europe. In the time when various European countries had colonies in Asia, the fashion standard was as pale as possible, with the occasional Asian element. The hierarchy among the mixed-bloods in the colony was based on this. That will now become different: the leading beauty standard will be Asian instead of white. The second-best ideal will be Asian mixed with a little white blood, which will include those of mixed blood, and then whites with a slight Asian influence (with or without the help of plastic surgery and make-up), and only then the rest. The European business community will increasingly choose models with ethnically ambiguous faces for their sales instrument, so that they can promote their products on the Asian market as well as to those Europeans who find Asians sexy (whether or not this has to do with the erotic appeal of power).

The Asian ideal of beauty will thus have its influence on the fashion industry, cosmetics, plastic surgery and personal care. All sorts of methods for artificially colouring the skin will appear and become big business, and the same will be true of colour rinsing. Slanted eyes will soon have greater status than straight eyes. This is a reversal of the current situation: in China, Singapore and other Asian countries, plastic surgery is now used to straighten slanted eyes. But in the coming decades this will change, as new pride and new self-respect take root as a result of the economic position of power.

Until then, hybrid, ethnically ambiguous beauty will be the order of the day. J-Lo is an example of this: she can be promoted in a variety of cultures simultaneously thanks to her multi-ethnic appearance. There are an increasing number of ethnically ambiguous models in both Asia and Europe. European companies now employ ethnically ambiguous models in Asia to promote their goods and services. Beauties from Asia have yet to break through in Europe. Do you know a single model from China? Yet very soon they will crowd the catwalks of Europe, and they may soon be used in European fashion outlets to attract Asian customers, or perhaps to please white Europeans? White European men traditionally find Asian women attractive. Mixed marriages between Europeans and Asians frequently consist of a European man and an Asian woman; the reverse is less frequent, except where Indian men are concerned. Employing Asian female models can thus be beneficial on a number of fronts.

Easternization

In addition to Asianization, Europe will also in the 21st century be confronted with Easternization, several aspects of which have already been mentioned in the previous chapter. Easternization means that increasing influence and economic strength and long-term investments will shift from Central to Eastern Europe, the area of the former Danube monarchy and all places farther eastwards. An increasing number of Western European companies are relocating their production capacity to Eastern Europe: the Czech Republic and Poland are the most popular countries, followed at some distance by Slovakia and Hungary. Opel and Volkswagen, Océ, Siemens and many other companies have moved their production to Eastern Europe, and publishers even have their books printed there – my previous book *Megatrends Nederland* was printed in Riga, Latvia.

After the fall of the Berlin Wall, a large market arose in Eastern Europe for Western products such as video recorders; there was a run on them immediately after "Die Wende". Knauf, the manufacturer of plasterboard and products derived from it, was the first company to invest in East Germany, Eastern Europe, and the Republic of Independent States. West European companies still export their products and services to Eastern Europe, for example

British Telecom (BT), which focuses on supplying IT and communications solutions to Eastern Europe through its offices in Hungary, the Czech Republic, Slovakia and Poland.

The same movement is noticeable in the other direction: highly trained people from Eastern Europe are coming to the West. There is, in fact, something of a brain drain. This is because education in Eastern Europe was traditionally of a very high level, as too were research and development programmes. In 1989 Bulgaria invested 2.5 per cent of its GDP in R&D, with an emphasis on microelectronics. Even today, Bulgarian higher education is still noted in rankings from the World Bank and the *Economist*: it is in fifth place in the world in the field of beta sciences and in eleventh place in the field of mathematics. Bulgarians head world tables in international IQ tests. But since 1989, much Bulgarian intellect has moved abroad. The R&D volume dropped from 2.5 per cent to just 0.5 per cent. The number of scientists involved in R&D dropped from 120,000 to 20,000, and the reduction was entirely due to the brain drain in the direction of the United States and Western Europe. Establishing high-tech companies in Eastern Europe, such as Nokia, which has set up a research centre employing 2000 personnel, could not stop this brain drain.

Some economists however are saying that many are now returning to their home countries, partly because Eastern Europe is now booming, thanks to increased tourism. They gain experience in the United States or Western Europe, where there is a better market for their knowledge and skills than in Eastern Europe, and return to their homelands with this experience when it becomes apparent that there is work for them there. "The booming situation has meant that highly

educated Eastern Europeans are moving back from Western Europe and settling here again," says Sevdalina Voynova, director of NDI, the National Democratic Initiative in the Bulgarian capital Sofia. "The poorly educated and the Roma (gypsies that do not have a good image in the Balkans) are moving away to Western Europe." This is a quality migration, in fact, which benefits Eastern Europe.

Trapped between the glory of the past and the vision for the future

Emil Kirjas

Maybe the best way to describe the widening generation gap that exists in Eastern Europe is with the title "Parents discover foreigners in their children"! Democracy has not only brought changes in the political systems of the nations that were suffering from the communist oppression. Many things have changed. Cities in the east of the old continent are no longer recognizable. Instead of the drab, grey buildings and the sad and worried faces of the people, a complete transformation has occurred: gleaming lights, fashionable attitude, vibrant atmosphere and above all, many people on the streets daily celebrating the newly found freedom. That outburst of dynamism is dominated by the younger generation – exactly those who brought the changes in their societies, but also those who, almost unaware of the dreadful past of their nation and parents, are aiming to bring even more changes in the future.

One of the smash hits of REM, the popular US band of the 1990s, was "Losing my religion". Somehow, in Eastern Europe, events have proved to be exactly the opposite of that song title. A new "religion" was found, a religion that preaches unity, prosperity and wealth for every nation on the old continent – with a very popular name: "the European Union". It has entered all parts of society, but only the young people have embraced it as a lifestyle. For the senior generation the belief in Europe is a mere expression of victory over suppression and a symbol of ending the European divide. The majority of the population still have glorious perceptions of the nation state, and expectations for state collective protection without much personal effort. Having understood that prosperity in the new world dominated by modern technology, computers and the Internet belongs to the individual and can be achieved only through a dynamic, competitive, courageous and accountable attitude, the new generation has created a cross-border lifestyle. That has contributed to a denial of national borders, the creation of competitive societies and a solid basis for the common European future. But it has created a new divide – one that will take time to overcome; a generation divide in society.

Young people simply don't accept any longer the preaching from the communist past where the future belonged to the youth. In a quest to be a European voice, the only acceptable alternative to the young generations is that they share the responsibility for the world of today.

Emil Kirjas is State Secretary of Foreign Affairs of Macedonia

A surprising group that is returning to Eastern Europe is made up of Israelis of Eastern European origin. Voynova comments:

> Israelis have an additional advantage. Many of Eastern European origin are now regaining the family fortune that they had once lost or the inheritances of relatives murdered

by the Nazis. Then you have a basis here. Often they can speak the language and they think it practical to invest in a virtually Muslim-free Eastern Europe, just in case things go radically wrong in the tumultuous Middle East.

That is, incidentally, why investments by trend-setting Jews and gays in Western Europe are also going eastwards. This can be seen clearly in Berlin and other parts of Germany. A Dutchman living in Germany said, "Germany is free of Moroccans, a blessing for the country. The Muslims here are Turkish, and they are good people who do not trouble you. Here my daughter can walk through the streets in a dress without being called a whore."

Young people in particular see the benefits that Eastern Europe currently has to offer. In Eastern Europe, there is a feeling among the young people which can be compared to that found among the youth in Western Europe during the period of rebuilding after the war. New chances have emerged after decades of communism. Old Stalinized generations have been removed; the young people have seized power.

Highly educated young people were politically active underground in the communist era: sometimes in a student movement, sometimes in forbidden radio stations and newspapers, sometimes in underground liberal/democratic parties. These politically involved young people have often played a vital role in the changes in their own country.

Young people in Eastern Europe have a strong orientation towards the European Union, to which they would like to belong, and set up cooperative ventures with their contemporaries abroad. They are reasonably at home with the European and American system of subsidies. In short: politically active young people in Eastern Europe are focusing their attention abroad. They consider individual "old" politicians as corrupt but do not turn away en masse from politics and government. They actively make use of their democratic rights, become active in (new) political associations, and often study law, economy and management instead of practical studies such as electronics. Being young and wanting to be involved in politics is nothing unusual in Eastern Europe, not even if you are a young woman. Young women are doing exceptionally well in Eastern Europe.

Young people in Eastern Europe are in addition active in NGOs; they even found them. Regularly, an NGO is founded in addition to a political youth organization, so that in this way the organization can be independent from the dithering mother party.

Liberalism is on the rise in Eastern Europe, but does not have the same meaning as in the West. Eastern Europeans couple liberalism largely with economic subjects, as well as with anti-corruption, human rights and the environment. Typical liberal subjects that are discussed in the West, such as homosexuality, abortion and euthanasia, can not yet be discussed in many former Eastern bloc countries.

There are many examples of young people in the Eastern bloc who have embarked on successful political careers. For example the mayor of Vilnius (the capital of Lithuania), Arturas Zuokas, is 35 years old. He is a member of one of the richest families in Lithuania (if not the richest), and lives in a magnificent house on the hills outside Vilnius, overlooking the city. His ancestry and wealth have never made him "suspect", probably because his family fortune was not obtained in political or governmental circles. Zuokas is not only a successful business man, he is well educated, a talented leader, very creative, and much loved by the inhabitants of the city. In no time he worked his way up through the ranks of the Lithuanian Liberal Union (which was a splinter group in the 1990s), and became its campaign manager. In 2000, largely thanks to his inspirational campaign, the LLU grew from one seat in the Lithuanian Parliament to 34. In one go, the LLU was suddenly the largest party. Zuokas could have remained in the party and probably would have been offered a cabinet post, but he chose, at the age of 31, to run for mayor of Vilnius. He won. In the past five years he has concentrated on rebuilding Vilnius, to impart an international and European allure to the city. And he has been successful, judging by the remarks of the World Mayor 2005 election:

> **Comment:** The Mayor has done outstanding work in Vilnius city and has promoted the city at various events and exhibitions. During his term the city image improved dramatically and the management of municipality was greatly improved.

> **Comment:** The Mayor is not afraid of innovation. Together with the citizens, he searches for new investments into the city. During the period he has been working, the city has changed its face 180 degrees. You should compare Vilnius with what it was five years ago – two different cities!

In Eastern Europe, the old politics are slowly but surely disappearing and the young are taking over. There are countless success

stories, but the one related here is typical. We shall hear a lot from Eastern Europe in the coming times. The Easternization of Europe is moving at full speed.

Islamization

On 12 June 1755 the faculty of philosophy of the University of Koningsbergen bestowed the title of doctor on Immanuel Kant. On the paper that was presented to Kant on that occasion is written in Arabic: "bismallah ar-rahman ar-rahim", which means "In the name of Allah, the Beneficent, the Merciful." That a young Prussian university (it was founded in 1544) should mention the first verse of the Koran on its diplomas demonstrates that it wished to be associated with a noble tradition that expressed itself in Arabic. Thus, in a remarkable way, attention was given to a language and a philosophy that was then associated with progressive thought. Islam at the time was inquisitive, tolerant, and offered considerable intellectual freedom. Researcher Oussama Cherribi (a lecturer at an American university, who calls himself Sam, because the name Oussama is not particularly popular in the United States) wrote that the sermons given in the mosques of 10th-century Damascus and Baghdad were much more liberal than those preached in the 20th-century mosques of Berlin, Copenhagen and Paris. Arabic was then the language of science, in Europe; even Jewish thinkers such as Maimonides wrote in Arabic, and Pope Silvester II learnt Arabic in 999 in order to understand science.

Koningsbergen is now called Kaliningrad. It would surprise me if official university documents still included a quote from the Koran. Arabic and Islamic thinking has fallen from grace, and the fundamentalist wahabi variant of Islam, originating in Saudi Arabia, has in fact colonized Islam in the 21st century.

Admittedly, there are some bright points. In the tumultuous and – since the dismantling of the Ottoman Empire – notoriously badly governed Middle East, there now seems more room for democracy (for instance in Lebanon). Twenty years before the fall of the Shah in Iran, when girls would walk happily through the streets of Teheran in mini-skirts, the American Islamic specialist Bernard Lewis predicted that the ayatollahs would seize power. He was ridiculed at the time, but has since been proved right. He advised President George W. Bush to start the war in Iraq and bring democracy to the country. Once again he drew ridicule, but again he has been proved right. The population of Iraq withstood the threats from fundamentalists and terrorists and went to the polling booths, and since then some bright points can be seen in the Middle East.

Despite this encouraging development, the Islamic world is still in tumult and strongly divided into a number of factions. Wahabi fundamentalists are fighting for power in various places: in the Middle East itself, with Saudi Arabia as the principal target; in Asia, for example in Indonesia where the government in fact is on a leash held by the fundamentalists, with the result that the country is becoming "Saudi-ized"; and in Western Europe where, since the 1960s, a large group of Muslims has settled. Some of these have found a good place for themselves in their new homes, but others are angry and want to take over power in Western European countries. Several Islamic specialists, including Bernard Lewis, but also Michael Scheur, predict that they will actually succeed: the West will lose the war against terrorism. According to Lewis, Europe will be governed by Muslims before the end of the 21st century, and will form Eurabia, together with North Africa (the Maghreb countries), as was discussed in the introduction.

Whether Eurabia will actually come into being or not, one phenomenon that will cause problems in Europe in the near future is the increasing Islamization of various cities, regions and countries. In France, around 10 per cent of the population is Muslim, in the United Kingdom around 3 per cent, in Belgium 1.8 per cent, and in the Netherlands 6 per cent. According to the French

Commission Stasi, there will be an Islamic majority living in the major Dutch cities by 2010. The Commission made a study trip to the Netherlands in 2004, and two of its members later stated that their experiences there had contributed to the fiercely controversial advice they gave the French government: to take drastic steps against the wearing of "ostentatious" religious symbols (headscarves) in French public schools. Following this advice, the French president, Jacques Chirac announced in December 2004 that there must "naturally" be a law about this. The announcement resulted in demonstrations by Muslims throughout the world.

Jacqueline Costa-Lascoux, a member of the delegation, said:

> The vast majority of Muslims in Western Europe are upright citizens. I have Islamic friends who have been imprisoned in their home countries because of their support for human rights. It is all about a clash with fundamentalism, politically inspired religious fanaticism. That is not civilization and I see the threats and dangers of it, and so I do not regret the conflict. On the contrary, it is about time for us to stand up for our rights.

She ascribes the situation to the paternalistic thinking which, according to her, has widely infiltrated left-wing Western European political parties. "The left is largely responsible for the disastrous failure of integration."

The Commission visited several countries, including the Netherlands where they concluded that integration had failed. They interviewed Muslims who stated that the Netherlands was the perfect place for the growth of Islamic fundamentalism and for preparing plans. The Netherlands is not a leading country in Europe, but it is interesting as a laboratory. What happens in this country is carefully monitored by the United States and other European countries, and is enough to cause unrest among the indigenous population and non-Islamic immigrants.

A survey carried out in the summer of 2004 by *De Volkskrant*, one of the most authoritative newspapers in the Netherlands, showed that only 14 per cent of the population had a positive image of Muslims. And that was before the murder by a Muslim fundamentalist of the Dutch filmmaker Theo van Gogh, which was perceived in the Netherlands as the Dutch equivalent of the attack on 11 September.

In Europe, it is generally not considered politically correct to research the image of minorities (we have our own traumas about that), but remarks in the media suggest that in other countries, for example Belgium and Denmark, Muslims also have a negative image. The media in virtually all Western European countries pays a lot of attention to Islam, to Islamic Europeans, and the problematical integration of large number of people in these groups in Europe.

It is rather amusing, then, to open a newspaper in Eastern Europe and discover that hardly anything at all is written about Muslims there. Of course, there are many countries in Eastern Europe that have no Muslims at all, so that makes a difference. Poland, the Czech Republic, Slovakia, the Baltic States, you name it: most of them are Muslim-free. Bulgaria has a large Turkish minority, dating back to the Ottoman period, but many Bulgarians of Turkish origin have left the country – some 1 million in all. There are still 1 million Turks in Bulgaria, a country with a total population of 8 million.

The majority of the Turkish diaspora in Europe causes fewer problems than other groups. In Belgium, France and the Netherlands there are large groups of Berbers from Morocco and Algeria. Berbers, descendants of the rulers of the famous Moorish Empire, which ruled large parts of Spain from Grenada, as well as other territories, do not have a very good reputation in Europe. There are a number of successful individual Berbers: writers, thinkers, artists, managers. They are ordinary Europeans, with nothing fundamentalist about them, liberal minded, often consuming alcohol, secular, and not at all intent on founding Eurabia. They look down with disdain on "stupid Muslims" who damage the image of all Muslims, either through backwardness, or because they have fallen into the grip of wahibi-ism – have become "Saudi-ized," in fact. "Saudi" is a favourite swear word that they use for "stupid Muslims". They find support among the progressive secular elite in Islamic countries, who share similar views.

Recently, a group of Moroccan career women from Rabat and Marrakech toured France to address French–Moroccan fundamentalist women about their "backwardness" and to spread the message that women in Moroccan cities are considerably more emancipated than the "Saudi-ized" Moroccan women in the diaspora. The tour had hilarious moments, but also bitter confrontations. Fundamentalism is taking hold of an increasing number of Muslims in Europe, certainly among the better educated. More and more headscarves can be seen on the streets, there are aggressive confrontations between fundamentalists and various other groups, and a fire is raging underground, although in most countries it is considered politically incorrect to mention it.

Muslims are not popular in Europe. The American research agency PEW held a survey in 17 countries: six Islamic countries, nine North American and European states, and India and China. This showed that 51 per cent of those questioned in the Netherlands had negative views about Muslims – the highest percentage. A comparable percentage felt that headscarves should be banned. The survey showed that Western Europe is largely negative about Muslims: 37 per cent of the Spanish and 34 per cent of the French see little good in them. In Asia China is the most negative, with 50 per cent. It is remarkable that in those countries where there is considerable fear for a Muslim terrorist attack, such as the United States and the UK, the majority have a positive image of Islamic people. In the UK only 14 per cent of the inhabitants have a negative view of Muslims. PEW notes that the survey was done before the Islamic suicide bombings in London on 7 July 2005. In the United States, only 22 per cent are negative. One remarkable conclusion was that the support for Muslim terrorism and for bin Laden is falling in Islamic countries.

Other surveys also show the low popularity of Muslims. A French survey showed that Jews in France now overwhelmingly vote for the Front National (FN) (which is not really enamoured of foreigners) because the FN has explicitly turned against the Muslims. Most of the anti-Semitic incidents in France are the work of Muslims, so this voting preference is hardly surprising. The FN used to be anti-Semitic; now it gratefully embraces the Jews. In Belgium, something similar is happening: Jews are now voting in large numbers for the Vlaams Belang, which is extremely anti-Islam. In Belgium too, the majority of anti-Semitic incidents are caused by Muslims. Here again, this new voting behaviour is not crazy. There too the party was initially anti-Semitic but rapidly adapted its position to attract the Jewish vote.

Euro-Muslims have a bad image not only among Jews, but also among non-Islamic immigrants from Africa and Asia, and among homosexuals, an important group in European cities. Gay-bashing has become a hobby of some groups of Islamic young men in various European countries. In Amsterdam, for many years the gay capital of Europe, according to a recent survey by the COC, the organization for gay integration, gays now only feel safe in the centre and southern district of the city (the latter mainly inhabited by whites, blacks, Latinos, Jews and Asians). In the eastern and western areas of the city, where Muslims are in the majority, they no longer feel safe. This feeling has only grown stronger since Chris Cain, chief editor of an American gay magazine, was beaten up in Amsterdam by a group of young Moroccan men.

Traditionally, homosexuals have been an economically prosperous and trend-setting group. Discussions with various solicitors and accountants in Amsterdam have indicated that gays and Jews in the city are currently transferring their long-term investments to safer, Muslim-free places. Others follow. A British

woman reported that her daughter in a mixed school had been beaten up by a group of Moroccan boys (average age, nine) because she was eating a cheese and ham sandwich (ham is pork, and Muslims do not eat that). Most such incidents are kept under wraps. The naïve multiculturalists who hold vital positions in most of these countries do not want to face this reality. But it is one of the most important reasons that so many middle-class people are leaving these cities and countries. The last census in the UK showed that 2 million young Brits had left the country.

For liberal Muslims, it is awkward to negotiate a course between the two extremes: liberal indigenous Europeans and conservative fellow Muslims. Jan Beerenhout, a Dutchman who converted to Islam in the 1950s, shakes his head:

> It is becoming increasingly difficult. Try to understand the situation. A group of Dutch emigrate to Morocco. We build a church there. We open a butcher's shop there that sells pork. We open a sex shop, because that's also part of our culture. We speak only Dutch, we wear clothes that reflect the style in our home country 60 years ago, and have no contact whatsoever with the local population. Do you think people in Morocco would accept that? But here, Moroccans do their thing in exactly this way. It is colonization and extremely repulsive. It has a negative influence on the image of Muslims in this country.

According to Beerenhout, many Muslims do not know the Koran at all but act as if they are devout believers. Take the headscarf:

> They say that the Koran says that women should wear a headscarf. That's nonsense. It doesn't say that at all. It says: Women, cover your jewels. This order was included because, at the time, many women in the Middle East were robbed of their jewellery, often the most valuable possession they had. In order to protect them, they were advised to cover their jewels. I was in Paris and visited a mixed sauna. There, among all the naked men and women, sat a naked woman reading an Arabic newspaper. I thought this remarkable, went up to her and asked whether Allah allowed this. She showed me her wrists, her ear lobes and her neck, and said: "You see, I'm not wearing any jewellery and therefore do not need to cover myself. Allah approves."

Declining congregations in mosques, no more mosques

The terrifying image for many people that Europe will soon be littered with mosques will not come about. Congregations in mosques are declining and will continue to decline, so plans for building more mosques in the future will be stopped. There is already an over-capacity in mosques, and the first bankruptcies of mosques are a fact. New technology will modernize old traditions. Young Muslims will use the Internet and cyber-imams for their religious devotions. A new trend has blown in from the Gulf States: you can receive an sms five times a day from the cyber-imam to remind you to think of Allah; there is no longer any need to be physically present in a mosque or to pray five times every day. Arranged marriages are also being modernized. In the Gulf States, if a Muslim mother wants to marry off her daughter to second-cousin X, the candidates first exchange email addresses and enter into a cyber relationship (including cyber sex) before they marry. This trend will undoubtedly be adopted by Muslims in Europe.

Conversions

The number of converts will increase: a small number of indigenous Europeans have already converted, reflecting what is already happening in the United States. In the US state of Texas there are now 500,000 Muslims, the majority of whom are ex-Christians from the lower class, converts who seek salvation in Islam, partly because of the strict separation of the roles of man and woman. In Europe, too, a growing number of indigenous people from the lower classes will convert to Islam, and traditionally converts are the greatest fanatics. That will also be the case here. Converts will play an important role in Muslim terrorism in Europe.

There will be two simultaneous trends among Muslim youth. Some will adopt a liberal interpretation of their faith or even turn their backs on it, eventually entering into mixed marriages and living in mixed neighbourhoods. These brave people will face difficulties: they will be distrusted by non-Muslims (who says that they aren't the human face of Al Qaeda?) and despised by fundamentalist Muslims, who will call them light Muslims. They will have leaders who will advise Euro Muslims not to wear headscarves, to keep their religion private and not to make it public, and will urge them to distance themselves from Al Qaeda and anti-Semitism.

Others will seek their salvation in fundamentalist Islam. This will grow in power and respectability. The fundamentalist Muslim preacher Abu Hamza al-Masri attracts packed mosques with his sermons filled with praise for suicide bombers and anti-Semitism. But as yet Muslim fundamentalism has not been translated into a political party. The first attempt in this direction – the AEL in Belgium – has, until now, had disappointing election results.

The Danish Queen Margrethe II, in her authorized

biography, calls on Europe to oppose all forms of radical Islam: "We have in recent years been issued a challenge by Islam, both nationally and internationally. It is a challenge we must take seriously. We have ignored the issue for too long, either because we were too tolerant or too lazy." According to the Queen, each of us must decide for ourselves whether we are tolerant "through indolence or conviction". In her biography the Queen says she accepts that people abroad will be indignant about her attitude. Denmark has been criticized internationally in recent years for its strict immigration and asylum policy. Margrethe voices the concern that many young dissatisfied Muslims will seek salvation in religion. "We cannot be satisfied with living next to each other, we must live together."

Nostradamus

The 16th-century visionary Nostradamus also said something about the future of Islam in Europe. In verse Century 5 Quatrain 74 he writes:

> From Trojan blood, the German heart will be born
> That will reach such levels of power
> That it will chase away the foreign Arabic people
> The Church will be raised again to its former glory.

Analysts believe that this prophecy refers to a strategic situation in which Muslim immigrants, independent of the question whether they have come for peaceful or violent ends, will be driven out under the influence of a single figure in Europe. Then the Christian church, which has been restricted in favour of Islam, will be restored to its former authority. Who the German with Trojan blood could be is unknown, but it could refer to a leader from the extreme right. In an earlier verse, mention is made of an exodus from France, which could refer to the banished Muslims.

The deep division about the place of Islam in Europe will continue and increase in the coming decades. As one white European businessman recently said, "If necessary, we'll all become Muslims. As long as we can still do our business." This brings Eurabia very close indeed.

Conclusion

Europe has always been something of a salad bowl. Thanks to relocations and a continuing migration flow, Europeans are used to the presence of those of other nationalities, religions, ethnicities. It has not always turned out well: several ethnic wars have flared up in the Balkans and in Northern Ireland there are still conflicts between Catholics and Protestants.

We are entering a new age in European history. A new European culture will emerge. The new Europe will know winners and losers, as the old Europe also had. The members of the white and immigrant (mostly Islamic) underclasses are initially losers, but they can become winners tomorrow in Western Europe, if their leaders succeed in mobilizing them for the cause of Eurabia. The rise of Asia will also influence Europe, and religion is back in the hearts of Europeans, both Christian and Islamic.

The present is always full of the future. On the streets in European cities in 2005 the future is already being created. We are heading towards turbulent times. Yet turbulence often creates new energy.

Islam: then and now

Vinco David

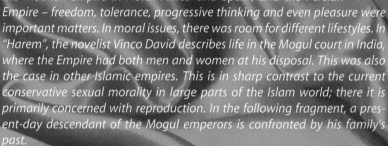

In the 21st century, Europe will suffer a lot from terrorism inspired by Al Qaeda, which is propagating with violence the wahabi variant of Islam to many, including European Muslims. Wahabi Islam is anti-West, anti-liberal, and rejects progressive thinking, many forms of art, and objective scientific practice. The wahabi Muslims market their message with the proposition that Islam formerly aspired to great heights because its leaders lived according to fundamentalist Islam. Nothing is further from the truth. In former Muslim empires that were successful – such as the Mogul Empire in India, the Ottoman Empire of Turkey and surrounding countries, the Moorish Empire in North Africa and Spain, and the Persian Empire – freedom, tolerance, progressive thinking and even pleasure were important matters. In moral issues, there was room for different lifestyles. In "Harem", the novelist Vinco David describes life in the Mogul court in India, where the Empire had both men and women at his disposal. This was also the case in other Islamic empires. This is in sharp contrast to the current conservative sexual morality in large parts of the Islam world; there it is primarily concerned with reproduction. In the following fragment, a present-day descendant of the Mogul emperors is confronted by his family's past.

Sydney takes me on a private tour through the museum. A lot of classical and European art that I have already become familiar with in England and Holland. But also some jewels from India, from the Mogul period. Sydney shows me several miniatures and tells me of their origin.

"The art form originated in Persia. The Indian Mogul emperors, who had strong cultural links with Persia, introduced the technique of painting miniatures into their court."

I pricked up my ears at the words "Mogul emperors".

Sydney continues: "The emperors were important patrons and gave artists every freedom. They even allowed the painters to depict living creatures, something that is forbidden in a strict interpretation of the Koran. Only Allah is allowed to create living creatures. It was precisely by ignoring this commandment that this art aspired to such high levels. The most beautiful portraits, palaces, and hunting scenes saw the light."

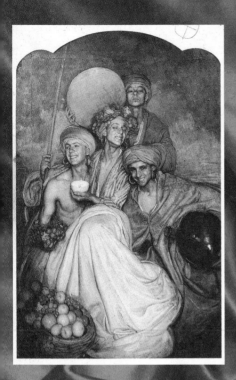

I eagerly absorb this information and admire Sydney's knowledge. We walk further.

I stop and look longer at one particular painting – not a miniature but one painted in a Western style. It shows a mosque in the marble palace in Agra. Agra, once the capital of the Indian Mogul Empire. And here in Malibu, I find a piece of history that is familiar to me. I study the painting carefully: the inner courtyard with a few believers, the decorated arches, the typical onion-shaped domes of the mosque. I recognize everything, even though I have never been there.

Sydney is delighted by my interest in the works he is showing me. He grasps my hand and whispers "my handsome prince" in my ear, and then gently bites it. He obviously meant well, but I am shocked by this public display of affection. I take my hand from his and look anxiously around. None of the other visitors in the room are paying any attention to us. Sydney smiles and tries to put me at ease. "I just wanted to let you know that I love you and that nobody here is offended by that."

Sydney doesn't have to convince me of his love for me, but I only partly believe what he says about offence. We are in a museum, not in the woods of Scheveningen. Sydney notices my reticence and tries a different tack. "I'll let you see that in your parts they didn't used to have a problem with showing love between men, and that they went a lot further than a swift caress of an earlobe."

I look at him with disbelief. "In any case, it's an insurmountable problem in my family, and in the past that would not have been otherwise."

Sydney continues to smile patiently. "I'll take you down to the storeroom in the basement. Down there there's stuff that even the Getty considers too confrontational to be exhibited in public. Come on."

Bemused, I follow Sydney. We take the service lift down to the basement. The storeroom is dimly lit and smells musty. There is nobody there. Sydney knows the way through the racks with paintings and other pieces of art like a blind man. He stops in front of a rack with a pile of folders. He reaches for one of them and starts carefully leafing through its contents. I look over his shoulder at what he is doing. They are Eastern miniatures, painted on paper. In the semi-darkness, I cannot see exactly what they depict. Then a grin appears on Sydney's face. He removes a miniature, but keeps the front hidden from me. He takes me to a table and turns on the light above it. I blink my eyes. Slowly Sydney turns over the sheet of paper and says dryly: "Mogul art, end of the sixteenth century."

What I see challenges my wildest fantasy about the Mogul period.

In front of me are two young men – one dark, one white – next to a fountain in a luxuriant garden. All they have on is a turban, each with a blue-green feather, and a cloth around their loins. One of the young men is sitting on the lap of the other and they are looking at each other, their red lips puckered in a kiss. Their arms caress each other's body. In the background there is a summer house surrounded by palm trees. Two pairs of legs protrude from the summer house; they are on top of each other, the lower pair with its feet upwards, the upper pair with its feet downwards. What is happening in the summer house is left to the imagination. Above the summer house, a pair of brightly-coloured birds are making a courtship flight. The whole is framed in golden paint.

I cannot keep my eyes off the fine lines and bright colours. The beauty of the young men and the scarcely disguised suggestion excite me. But I am also confused. Is this Mogul art, art from an Islamic empire? That is surely impossible. It is as if Sydney is reading my thoughts. "It is a distinct possibility that the Mogul emperor also enjoyed this. As far as I can tell, it comes from the imperial palace in Agra. In any case it is authentic. It has been authenticated by other specialists."

Vinco David is a political scientist and works in the financial services industry. He has written various business books, articles and essays, as well as children's stories. This is an extract from his novel The Male Harem, *published in Dutch by Van Gennep Publishers in Amsterdam, www.vangennep-boeken.nl*

Conclusion

The 21st century will be important in the development of Europe. There are many favourable signs. Europe can continue to play an interesting role in the new economic order that will emerge in the 21st century. It will do so without hegemony, but we took leave of that in the 19th century, when the United States became the leader of the Western world. A new country, in a different continent, populated by European emigrants (often from the lower European classes), mixed with other ethnic groups, became the leader of the West and remained so throughout the 20th century. In the 21st century, the United States will have to share world supremacy with Asia. In the near future, the world will have not one, but six economic superpowers, and three of those will be in Asia: China, India and Japan. Although they are naturally rivals to each other (just as, within Europe, France, the United Kingdom and Germany are each other's rivals), they will in many cases operate together and cooperate.

Economically, Asia will in this century become a powerhouse, and that has consequences for Europe. In Europe, prosperity need not be put under pressure by these new economic power relationships in the world. There will still be sufficient ways of earning money, for example, with tourism and "fun". Europe is attractive for large numbers of tourists from Asia.

The ageing of Europe's population not only poses problems, but also offers opportunities: for the care industry, for care tourism, wellness, and tourism for seniors within the continent. There are also threats: the cost of pensions has to be coughed up. The technological revolution will bring a lot of good, but also many new dangers. At the same time, the technological revolution will bring new moral dilemmas. Who, in the future, will decide whether a pensioner with dementia should be given a new pacemaker or a plastic hip? Who decides which criminal should have a chip that prevents criminal behaviour implanted in his brain? Who decides whether euthanasia should be allowed in cases of dementia? Security will become a major issue, certainly as terrorism increases. Religion and spirituality are back after a time in the wilderness, and the conflict with Islam will intensify. That will cause tensions and might perhaps result in a new divide in Europe.

On a day in 2025, a European radio could broadcast a news bulletin something like this:

> Good morning, here is the news for 3 January 2025.
>
> The European security services have prevented bombing attacks on a number of European high-speed train routes. The German intelligence service intercepted a telephone call from a Dutch–Belgian Islamic extremist group. The attack was planned to take place on New Year's Eve. The terrorists had intended to detonate explosions simultaneously on high-speed trains carrying partygoers into the stations of Frankfurt, London, Copenhagen, Amsterdam, Brussels and Rome. If they had succeeded, it would have caused the deaths of tens of thousands of people, the Ministry of Justice announced today. Later today, the Ministry will be holding a press conference. The planned attack illustrates the growing tension in the Western part of the European Union, where Muslim fundamentalists are trying to seize power so that they

can split off this part of Europe and unify it with Northern Africa into Eurabia.

Today the French city of Marseille, following the example of the British city Bradford, introduced the sharia. From today, Islamic law will apply throughout the city.

In Bulgaria, the country's tenth atomic power plant was opened today. The country is now totally independent of oil from the Middle East for its energy needs. Last year Hungary achieved the same status.

Rising sea levels have resulted in several parts of the southern Netherlands and northern Belgium being abandoned, it was officially announced today. The sea has already reclaimed these areas of land. Yesterday, the few remaining inhabitants were evacuated and taken to higher ground.

Today a conclave of cardinals is meeting in the Vatican City for the election of a new pope. It is generally thought that the new pope will be from either South America or Asia, two areas where Catholicism is growing rapidly. In Europe too, Catholicism is witnessing a revival. This is true of both classical Catholicism and evangelical Catholicism, which is largely organized outside official church institutions, is mainly led by women, and is mixed with religions and other spiritual movements.

In the local elections that were held yesterday in Great Britain, Germany, Austria, Italy and Romania, the national parties for the elderly achieved an absolute majority. Between 55 and 70 per cent of the votes were given to these parties, which thus strengthened their grip on power. The parties now supply 60 per cent of all elected mayors in these countries.

The merged HSBC-Deutsche Bank has announced that it will be moving its head office from London to Shanghai. The main focal point of the bank's activities is now in Asia, according to a statement explaining the move. Earlier, the

Banque Paribas ABN AMRO and More Bank (the merger between Lloyds TSB, Banco Santander and Credit Suisse) both announced that they were moving their headquarters to the Indian capital Delhi, for similar reasons.

In the south of Italy, a new tourist attraction was opened today, aimed at Asian and older North-West-European tourists. In a newly reconstructed Roman city, which offers full invalid access and where all signs are in five languages, including English, Hindi and Mandarin Chinese, all visitors

will wear togas as they tour the city. A wellness centre has been constructed next to it.

European Commissioner Ayaan Hirsi Ali yesterday opened the new Sun City for senior citizens, built on the border between Germany and the Netherlands. In this Christian city, where the youngest inhabitant is 65 and the oldest 112, there are no police officers. Neighbourhood watches, together with security cameras and robot security drones, guarantee the inhabitants' safety.

Sport. He's 53 years old and he's finally made it. Zinedine Zidane has been appointed trainer of the French football team. Last week it was announced that Johan Cruyff, who is now 78, had been appointed trainer of the Dutch national team and that the 80-year-old Franz Beckenbauer had been named national coach of the German team.

The weather. Cloudy and periods of rain in Northern Europe. Temperature around 14 degrees. Dry and sunny in Southern Europe, with temperatures of 20 degrees.

Traffic news: in common with the last few months, there are no hold-ups on the roads. It is, however, busy in the air. Travellers should expect a two-hour delay between Berlin and Torremolinos, Stockholm and Nice, and between Brussels and Sofia.

This was the news for 3 January 2025.

References

Alonso, S., "Dit wordt Europa's meest open economie", *NRC Handelsblad*, 29 April 2005.

Armstrong, K., *Holy War*. New York City, 2001.

Armstrong, K., *The Battle for God*. New York City, 2000.

Austen, S., *De Europese culturele ambitie*. The Hague, 2005.

Bakas, A., *Megatrends Nederland*. Schiedam, 2005.

Bakas, A., *Nieuw Nederland: Marketing en de demografische revolutie*. Schiedam, 2004.

Bakas, A. *et al.*, *De dag ontsluierd*. The Hague, 2003.

Barschot, J. van. "De Europese stoel wordt veel te duur'", *NRC Handelsblad*, 3 March 2005.

Beck, D., *Spiral Dynamics*. Oxford, 2004.

Bistrup, A., *Margrethe*. Copenhagen, 2005.

Boekestijn, A. J., "Osmaanse weemoed", *Binnenlands Bestuur*, 14 January 2005.

Bolkestein, F., *The limits of Europe*. Tielt, 2004.

Bouma, J. D. "Het grote genieten", *NRC Handelsblad*, 25 September 2004.

Brouwer, A., "De bom van Khan", *De Groene Amsterdammer*, 28 February 2004.

Cleveland, H., *Nobody in Charge: Essays on the future of leadership*. 2002.

Colijn, K., "De alomtegenwoordige vijand slaat toe", *Vrij Nederland*, 9 April 2005.

Corte, S. de. *Het bergdorp in de overgang*. Amsterdam, 2005.

Cowell, A., "Oslo boort pensioenfonds aan", *NRC Handelsblad*, 4 January 2005.

Creveld, M. van. *The Transformation of War*. Jerusalem, 1991.

Crichton, M., *State of Fear*. Harper Collins, New York City, 2004.

D'Souza, D., *The End of Racism*. New York City, 1995.

Das, R. en R., *Future Flashes*. Baarn, 2004.

Das, R. en R., *Visions of the Future: A new golden age for the low countries*. Baarn, 1999.

Djavann, C., *Bas les voiles*. (*Take off the veil*.)Paris, 2004.

Duijvesteijn, H. H. *et al.*, *Voorbij label en lifestyle: Jongerenmarketing in volwassen perspectief*. The Hague, 2004.

Ewijk, C. van *et al.*, *Vergrijzing als uitdaging.* The Hague, 2003.

Fallaci, O., *Anger and Pride.* Rome, 2002.

Ferguson, R., *Colossus.* New York, 2004.

Ferraresi, P. M. *et al.*, *Unequal Welfare States: distributive consequences of population ageing in six European countries.* Rome, 2005.

Friedman, T., *The World is Flat.* New York, 2005.

Fukuyama, F., *State Building.* Washington, 2004.

Fukuyama, F., *The End of History and the Last Man.* Washington, 2003.

Gogh, Th. van. *Allah weet het beter.* Amsterdam, 2004.

Golder, T. J. *et al.*, *Mondiale revoluties.* The Hague, 2003.

Gray, J., *Al Qaeda and What it Means to be Modern.* London, 2003.

Greenfield, S., *Tomorrow's People: How 21st-century technology is changing the way we think and feel.* 2003.

Groenewold, Dost. S. *et al.*, *Koffie Verkeerd 2: Intercultureel management in praktijk.* Lelystad, 1995.

Haass, R.N., *The Opportunity: America's moment to alter history's cause.* Washington, 2005.

Hirsi Ali, A., *De zoontjesfabriek.* Amsterdam, 2004.

Huntington, S., *Who are We.* Riverside, 2004.

Huntington, S., *The Clash of Civilizations and the Remaking of World Order.* Riverside, 1998.

Imber, C., *The Ottoman Empire.* New York, 2002.

Jeu, J. de., *Gezondheidszorg in 2020.* Amersfoort, 2004.

Jordan, M., *Nostradamus and the New Millennium.* London, 1998.

Kerr, A., *Lost Japan.* Sydney, 2003.

Lachmann, G. *Tödliche Toleranz. Die Muslime und unsere offene Gesellschaft.* Munich, 2005.

Lamb, R., *Tien trends.* Leiden, 2004.

Laroui, F. "Kunnen moslims denken?" *Vrij Nederland*, 16 April 2005.

Leijendekker, M., "Jeremy Rifkin: Europe moet geloven in zijn eigen droom", *NRC Handelsblad*, 12 March 2005.

Leonard, M. *Why Europe will Run the 21st Century.* London, 2004.

Lewis, B., *What Went Wrong? The clash between Islam and modernity in the Middle East.* London, 2002.

Lewis, Bernard, *The Crisis of Islam: Holy war and unholy terror.* London, 2003.

Lutz, P. and Obersteiner, E., *Megatrends Osteuropa.* Vienna, 2004

Manji, I., *The Islam Dilemma.* Toronto, 2004.

Meadows, D., *The Limits to Growth.* Club of Rome, 1972.

Mehta, S., *Maximum City.* Mumbai, 2005.

Menzies, G., *1421: The year China discovered the world.* New York, 2004.

Mesters, B., "Paraderen langs de afgrond", *NRC Handelsblad,* 26 February 2005.

Naipaul, V. S., *India: A million mutinies now.* London, 2000.

Naisbitt, J., *Megatrends 2000.* New York City, 2000.

Naisbitt, J., *Megatrends Asia.* New York, 1999.

Naisbitt, J., *Megatrends.* New York City, 1989.

Napoleoni, L. *Modern Jihad: Tracing the dollars behind the terror networks.* London, 2004.

Noorhaidi, A., *Laskar Jihad-Islam: Militancy and the quest for identity in post-New Order Indonesia.* Utrecht, 2005.

Nye, Joseph, *The Paradox of American Power: Why the world's only super power can't do it alone.* 2002.

Osch, B. van. "Winter aan de Costa is Hollandser dan Holland", *Elsevier,* 18 December 2004.

Pilny, K., *Das Asiatische Jahrhundert: China und Japan auf dem Weg zur neuen Weltmacht.* Frankfurt, 2005.

Posthumus, A., *Een comfortabele oude dag in Oost-Europa.* Amsterdam, 2004.

Quataert, D., *The Ottoman Empire 1700–1922.* Cambridge, 2000.

Raat, F. de. "Bakstenen verzilveren", *NRC Handelsblad,* 26 February 2005.

Rashid, A., *Taliban: Militant Islam, oil, and fundamentalism in Central Asia.* London, 2000.

Rees, M., *Our final century.* London, 2003.

Ridder, W. de, *Koers 2020: Een gouden decennium in het verschiet.* The Hague, 2004.

Ridder, W. de. *De strijd om de toekomst.* The Hague, 2003.

SCP, *In het zicht van de toekomst – Sociaal en Cultureel Rapport 2004.* The Hague, 2004.

Smit, W., *Globalisering: Zegen of vloek?* 2005.

Steketee, H., "Britten wacht oude dag met zorgen", *NRC Handelsblad,* 13 October 2004.

Steketee, H., "Ook in Italië zijn pensioenen te luxe", *NRC Handelsblad,* 29 July 2004.

Schilperoord, P., *Techniek van de toekomst.* Diemen, 2004.

Susskind, L. and Zion, L., "Can American democracy be improved?" Draft working paper of the Consensus Building Institute and the MIT-Harvard Public Dispute Program, 2002.

Stasi, B., *Commission de Reflexion sur l'application du principe de laïcité dans la Republique.* Paris, 2004.

Tamminga, M., "Europeanen vechten al jaren voor hun pensioen", *NRC Handelsblad,* 2 October 2004.

Tenner, E., *Why Things Bite Back: Technology and the revenge of unintended consequences.* New York City, 1996.

United Nations. *Millenium Ecosystem Assessment.* New York City, 2005.

Veer, P. van der, "Religie is juist modern", *De Volkskrant,* 4 September 2004.

Verrips, T., *Living Tomorrow.* Amsterdam, 2004.

Vloemans, A., *Politeia: Geschiedenis van de sociaal-politieke filosofie.* The Hague, 1980.

Weeda, F., "Superforenzen", *NRC Handelsblad* 6 March 2005.

Wheatcroft, A., *Infidels: A history of the conflict between Christendom and Islam.* London, 2005.

Wilde, R. de. *De voorspellers; een kritiek op de toekomstindustrie.* Amsterdam, 2000.

Wilson, D. and Purushothaman, R., *Dreaming with BRIC's: The path to 2050.* Goldman Sachs, 2003.

Websites

www.smo.nl
www.europa.eu.int/comm/eurostat
www.economist.com/surveys
www.cia.gov
www.esa.un.org/unpp
www.worldbank.org
www.world-tourism.org
www.ebrd.com
www.esa.un.org/unpp
www.trendwatching.com
www.spiraldynamics.info
www.escador.com
www.activityinternational.nl
www.economist.com
www.wto.org
www.chinanet.be
www.migrationinformation.org

Photo credits

Ronald Brakel (1, 7, 16, 19, 59, 242/243a), Avi Goodall (36, 149, 238), Mark Janssen (8), Keiko Goto (204), Adjiedj Bakas (40a and b).

Christopher Poliquin (2), Mary Ann Madsen (22), Richard Gunion (26), Helmut Watson (32), Roman Milert (56), Angelo Gilardelli (61), Pauline Vos (63), Nick Stubbs (68), Steven Pepple (72/73, 139), Radovan Kraker (77), Martina Misar (79), Marco Kopp (81), Kristian Peetz (91), Tom McNemar (93), Rob Bouwman (100), Vaide Seskauskiene (112), Scott Rothstein (117, 176), Duпan Zidar (118/119), Jo Ann Snover (130), Olga Telnova (136), Kirsty Pargeter (145), Nadezda Pyastolova (154), Stephane Tougard (157), Sascha Burkard (158/159), Linda Bucklin (160), Laurin Rinder (167, 219), Franziska Lang (179), Hermann Danzmayr (190), Han Csernoch (191), Han Sheng Chin (193), Nicholas Sutcliffe (200/201), Steve Lovegrove (208), Danijel Micka (210), Beata Pastuszek (217), Phil Date (222, 223), Andre Nantel (229a), Simon Gurney (229b), Nicholas Monu (230), Sue Colvil (236/237), Peter Gustafson (241), Irene Teesalu (246), Erik de Graaf (252), Randy McKown (262), Wang Sanjun (265), all at Dreamstime.com.